Handmade Holiday

FESTIVE EMBROIDERY PATTERNS AND TECHNIQUES FOR CHRISTMAS CRAFTING

ALYSSA PLOOF

rockynook

Handmade Holiday

Festive Embroidery Patterns and Techniques for Christmas Crafting
www.etsy.com/shop/ByAlyPloof

Project editor: Maggie Yates
Project manager: Lisa Brazieal
Marketing coordinator: Katie Walker
Copyeditor: Maggie Yates
Layout: Danielle Foster
Cover and interior design: Kim Scott, Bumpy Design

ISBN: 979-8-88814-229-5
1st Edition (1st printing, October 2024)
© 2024 Alyssa Ploof
All images © Alyssa Ploof

Rocky Nook Inc.
1010 B Street, Suite 350
San Rafael, CA 94901
USA

www.rockynook.com

Distributed in the UK and Europe by Publishers Group UK
Distributed in the U.S. and all other territories by Publishers Group West

Printed in China

To my parents, who have always encouraged me
to pursue a career that brings me joy.

To both of my grandmas, who instilled in me a love of
working with my hands and creating handmade treasures.

And to all of you who take the time
to work away at my embroidery patterns.

Thank you for supporting me in making
this dream of creating for a living a reality.

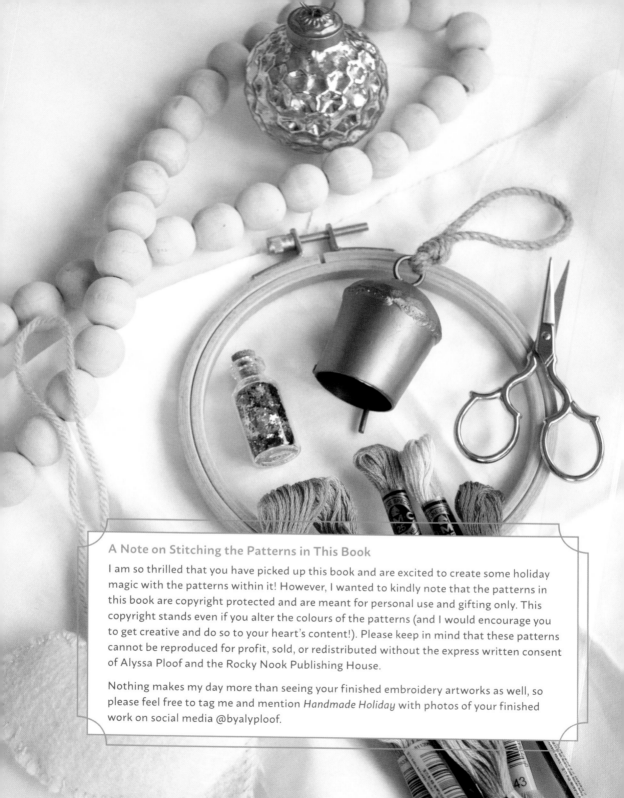

A Note on Stitching the Patterns in This Book

I am so thrilled that you have picked up this book and are excited to create some holiday magic with the patterns within it! However, I wanted to kindly note that the patterns in this book are copyright protected and are meant for personal use and gifting only. This copyright stands even if you alter the colours of the patterns (and I would encourage you to get creative and do so to your heart's content!). Please keep in mind that these patterns cannot be reproduced for profit, sold, or redistributed without the express written consent of Alyssa Ploof and the Rocky Nook Publishing House.

Nothing makes my day more than seeing your finished embroidery artworks as well, so please feel free to tag me and mention *Handmade Holiday* with photos of your finished work on social media @byalyploof.

Contents

Introduction

THE FIRST THING YOU'LL NOTICE about the embroidery patterns in this book are the colours. Sorting through the millions of coloured pencils, tubes of paint, and eventually, bobbins of coloured embroidery floss has always been the most beloved part of the creation process for me. It's what started me on the path to becoming an artist.

Anybody who knows me well will tell you that I have just a smidge of artistic talent that began with afternoons at my grandparent's house, spent drawing and colouring in artworks for my grandma's fridge. I took the greatest care an 8-year-old possibly could in selecting all the prettiest colours and was filled with so much pride when my grandma displayed them proudly. Those afternoons also ignited in me a lifelong pull to constantly be creating something. It felt like creating was always going to be an intrinsic part of who I am. For a long time that meant creating more of my prized drawings and, eventually, paintings. I even went as far as attending art school to further explore my passion for creating. But after graduating, I was left with a strong sense of "What now?"

I had polished all of my technical creating skills, yet I didn't know what to create next and where I fit as an artist in this world.

One day, a few years after graduating, I was exploring one of the gift shops in my city that prided themselves on featuring local artists and makers. I came across a handful of embroidered hoop artworks on the wall and marvelled at their silky floss shining in the soft shop lights. I was immediately intrigued with this reimagined art form that had an elevated texture and uniqueness to it. At the time, I didn't know that it would become such a huge part of my life; it was just nice to see something that reignited that creative appreciation in my heart. A short while later, a couple of my best friends started practicing embroidery to keep busy while the world slowed down. One of them later gifted me an embroidered bike for my birthday that meant a lot to me and pushed me to finally try my own hand at embroidery.

That first year of practicing embroidery was incredibly humbling, but also quite creatively fulfilling, to say the least. As someone who has a knack for picking up creative things fairly easily, embroidering was something that took great patience and practice to get better at. Now, after having practiced the art form for three years, here's a piece of advice I'm happy to pass along to you: Whether you're just starting out on your embroidery journey or a seasoned stitching pro, there will always be days when you poke yourself a million times, need to cut out your work, or put down your hoop after an hour of work only accomplished a single flower.

In those initial days of trial and error, the process was new, and the materials of floss, cotton, and wood felt special. Doodling a design to stitch on the fabric felt like a breath of fresh air.

Eventually, after that first year of creating my own designs and following a bunch of other inspiring embroidery artists on social media, I released my first original embroidery pattern in my newly minted Etsy shop: a Christmas wreath. It felt scary and new to release it after only posting a few of my original embroidery artworks. My dad was my first customer (he bought a handful of my hoops as Christmas gifts for the neighbours). I tried my hand at pattern writing again a few months later. I've always had a love of florals and I really leaned into that when creating new embroidery patterns. I even started dreaming up crafting patterns of other objects made of florals, which you'll soon see later in this book. Long story short, I kept writing patterns, honing my embroidery skills, and sharing them with my embroidery community on social media. As time went on, my embroidery career, pattern shop, and social media following grew, which led to new and exciting opportunities. One such opportunity is being able to release this book of Christmas patterns to all of you.

The other thing you should know about me is that I love a theme. It's one of the major reasons I love a holiday and the joy that sparks a ton of creation when it comes to my embroidery patterns. One of my busiest times of the year are the months of September through December, when everybody is packing away their sun loungers for fairy lights and hunkering down for the colder, cozier months. That's when embroidery patterns have their time to shine! And what is more thoughtful and special then crafting and creating gifts for loved ones leading up to the holidays? It's why I start doodling candy canes during mid-August and stitching up holiday patterns before the leaves have even turned golden. It's why I'm so excited to share this book of patterns with all of you.

I hope that stitching these patterns brings you that same joy that I felt while creating them. This book is full of cozy and classic Christmas designs that are sure to keep you festive for a good while. The book is full of all the stitching wisdom I've picked up over the last few years and poured out for you to utilize on your own embroidery journey. It has been a pleasure to share my passion with you. My last hope is that in stitching these designs, you feed that creative joy that exists in all of us. It's one of the most special parts of being a human, in addition to being able to make things with our hands. And don't forget to pass along that magic to your loved ones, too.

Happy Holidays,

Close up of the various colours and stitches on this festive pattern.

CHAPTER 1

The Art Of Embroidery

THE MAGIC OF EMBROIDERY is that it's such a slow process. Every stitch is another step toward that finished piece. Although there's nothing like the pride you feel of displaying or gifting your finished piece, the patience-testing practice of carefully stitching in colours is a reminder that growing and creating things takes time and perseverance. Below are some of the benefits of practicing this artform, in addition to some helpful tips to remember as you're stitching!

THE BENEFITS OF EMBROIDERY

- The methodical nature of practicing embroidery encourages peacefulness and a slower pace while creating. This can be super effective for mental health and wellness!

- Much like reading a book or playing music, embroidery allows you to take a break from screen time, while also encouraging you to still engage your brain with the creative process. If you find the process too quiet, a lot of artists like to put on audio books or music to listen to while stitching!

- Embroidery is an easy art form to pick up and put down and relatively mess free…aside from all those extra thread snippings! This makes it easy to work in your free time and pick up where you left off.

- Embroidery is a relatively cost-effective craft that features a wide range of flexible, colourful, and handmade materials to use and work with. There are so many floss colours to choose from, in addition to a range of fabrics, hoops, accessories, and more.

HELPFUL TIPS

If you're new to embroidery, here are some basic knowledge, tips for use, and best practices.

- The most important embroidery tip I can give you is to always be mindful of your fabric's tension. It will make a world of difference when you're transferring and stitching your pattern. I'll detail how to achieve a good fabric tension in the Pattern Transferring Methods and Starting Your Project sections later on!

- When pulling your working thread from an incased bundle of DMC Floss, pull from the side with the number of the colour code on it. This will make pulling out your desired length easier. I would also recommend winding your floss on bobbins, if possible, to keep the left-over floss from getting tangled or knotted. This is completely a personal preference!

- When pulling out floss to stitch with, I typically measure about two feet (61 cm). This length mostly prevents the floss from getting tangled.

- If your floss gets knotted while stitching, most times it's easier to cut the thread at the knot and start fresh, but you can also use your needle to carefully unpick it. Even the most skilled embroidery artists get tripped up by floss knots, so don't spend more than a minute trying to unwind them! Simply snip off the end of the floss at the knot, tie another knot in your left-over thread (or start with a new piece of floss) and restart your stitching where you left off.

- Utilize your needle like a handy little brush/editing tool to gently straighten loose or curvy satin stitching, to adjust the circular shapes of your French knots, and to gently pull whipped back stitches into the exact place you want it. Just remember to be gentle with it, so you're not breaking the threads with your needle tip. Your needle can be extra helpful in accomplishing a neat and beautifully stitched finished piece.

- The embroidery floss colours used in the patterns of this book are already pre-chosen for your convenience, but if you do decide to venture off by choosing your own colour palettes (or even for future projects), my best advice is to always choose your colours in broad daylight! This will help you see the colour in its purest form and will save you from a regretful morning of cutting out your work after a long night of stitching with colours that aren't quite right.

EMBROIDERY TOOLS

If you've picked up this book and have decided to become an embroidery artist, the first thing you'll need to get started is a well-stocked kit of embroidery tools. The great news is that building one out is a really fun and satisfying process (but truly, when is buying craft supplies not super fun?). When I was first starting out, I asked a lot of questions: Where do I begin to look for supplies? What type of fabric should I use? What even is an embroidery hoop? Can I use regular scissors instead of embroidery scissors? What's the difference between embroidery floss and other threads? In this section, I'll break down all my knowledge and recommendations for what you'll need to create top-notch embroidery artworks!

Embroidery Floss

Embroidery floss (**FIGURE 1.1 A**) is the technical term for six strands of cotton thread made up into one piece of "floss." Most embroidery artists will take these six strands and separate them when stitching to yield different results. For example, I'll often use three strands when stitching most satin stitches or fine detail work, but six strands for working on French knots or woven roses. A common French brand called DMC is carried in most craft and fabric stores and one you'll see used in the later patterns in this book!

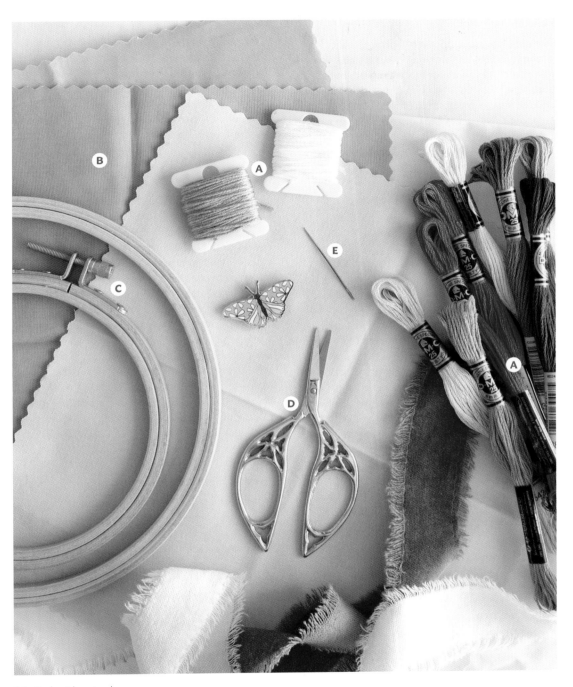

1.1 *Embroidery tools*

Fabric

The next biggest supply you'll need to collect is a fabric surface to stitch on (**FIGURE 1.1 B**). I'll go into greater detail about fabric later on, but I'll note here that you'll want a fabric with a tight enough weave (meaning the threads of the fabric are close together) to hold your stitches securely. If you're creating artworks specifically in the hoop, you'll also want to cut a square of fabric with 2" of room around your hoop size so the hoop has fabric to grip. For example, a 6" hoop will need an 8" piece of fabric.

Embroidery Hoops

An embroidery hoop (**FIGURE 1.1 C**) is going to be your best friend when it comes to working on any type of embroidery. Its primary purpose is to hold the fabric taut while you're working on it and the resulting fabric tension makes a world of difference when you're stitching. One of the biggest rules in embroidery is to keep your fabric as taut as possible (as it will keep your stitches straight and smooth), and a good embroidery hoop will do just that. When I first started stitching, I picked up whatever hoops that I could find, which happened to be light wood, silver-clasped bamboo hoops that are readily available at most craft stores. These hoops worked for a while and are a good cost-effective option for beginners, but as I've gone on, I've come to prefer gold-clasped beech wood hoops or plastic Elovell hoops. These are a little harder to find, but can be found in some shops on Etsy and by sites like Nurge.net. I look for hoops with a gold screw-clasp that can be tightened with a screwdriver (this can be a game changer).

Embroidery Scissors (Snips)

Embroidery scissors (**FIGURE 1.1 D**) are good for more than just looking cute on your desk.

If you've seen these tiny scissors at the craft store before, maybe you've wondered how they differ from normal scissors. Their main capability is being sharp and small enough to cut floss cleanly, but they are also a workhorse when you need to cut out some wonky satin stitches or a French knot pulled too tight! You can find these at most craft or fabric shops, or even more easily on Etsy.

Needles

When I first started, I really didn't think about what kind of needle (**FIGURE 1.1 E**) would be best for embroidery specifically, I just thought any old needle would do. It turns out whatever needle you use truly is personal preference, and each artist likely has their own go-to sizes and styles of needles. After a few years of trying out these different types of needles (there's embroidery, tapestry, chenille, milliners, beading) I've come to settle on my personal go-to: A size 5 embroidery needle by DMC. I find this needle has the ideal eye size (meaning the hole at the top of the needle) to use for working with both three and six strands of floss. These can be found at most craft or fabric stores. Try out some different needle styles and see which type best suits you!

Pencil / Heat Erasable Pen

When I first started designing my own original embroidery artworks, I used to freestyle draw my designs by hand with a regular lead pencil straight onto the fabric. I used this same method for years and made sure to cover any pencil marks with my stitches. I can vouch that this method definitely works, but a game changer was using a heat erasable pen. You can find these at most craft or department stores, and I would recommend trying the FriXion brand of heat erase pens. You can easily erase the lines after stitching with a hair dryer or an iron.

Optional

Needle Minder

Needle minders are essentially aesthetically shaped pins with a strong magnet attached to catch and hold your needle when you're not actively stitching. They're super handy so you're not always sticking your needle in the nearest pillowcase or jean pocket.

Needle Threader

Needle threaders are handy little tools used to help thread your floss through the eye of the needle. You can find them at most craft and fabric shops.

Thimble

A thimble is a useful little tool to help protect you from damaging your fingertips with constant needle poking. They are especially helpful when stitching through two layers or thicker fabric, and especially when you're stitching cross knots close together in the center of a flower.

Fabric Scissors

You can certainly use regular scissors when cutting out squares of fabric, but fabric scissors will make it a bit easier, especially when cutting thicker fabrics. Alternatively, you can buy an Olfa-brand fabric cutter.

Pinking Shears

Pinking shears will allow you to cut a zig-zag edge around your fabric squares to keep the edges from pulling and fraying. This won't stop pulling or fraying completely, but will help slow down the process while you're working on your project. Alternatively, you can buy an Olfa pinking blade for their fabric cutters.

SELECTING FABRIC FOR EMBROIDERY

Whether you've decided to stitch your embroidery artwork as a permanent, in-hoop artwork or on a loose garment like a tea towel or sweater, choosing your fabric type is an important consideration. It'll make all the difference when you're stretching it in a hoop and stitching the project. You'll also need to consider the weave (meaning how close together the threads of the fabric are), texture, and opacity of the fabric. This will affect how your finished embroidered project comes out—and let me tell you, after you spend several hours working away at a project, you'll thank yourself for taking the time to select the right fabric.

When I first started out, I did a little bit of research and choose a basic cotton to stitch on, as I knew it had a tight weave and would be ideal for stretching and holding embroidery floss securely. What I didn't consider was that the white cotton was thin enough that you could see the darker floss through the fabric. Although it wasn't terribly noticeable, it did leave a less-finished look. Since then, whenever I'm using a white or cream linen, I will likely always double the fabric squares for a more opaque and clean background.

Another time I wanted to stitch a floral design on a stretchy, low-cost cotton t-shirt and found it was a tricky fabric to stretch in the hoop. Once I had it taut enough, I stitched away and was super pleased with the finished design. But low and behold, once I took the design out of the hoop the fabric shrunk and puckered around the design and left me less than thrilled. This isn't to say there aren't thicker, higher-quality cotton t-shirts that are perfectly suited to embroidery; it's just a lesson on choosing the right fabric for embroidering. I hope to save you from these pitfalls when you're committing to embroidering a beautiful, finished project!

In terms of fabrics I do recommend, I often stick with natural fabrics with a tight weave, namely higher-quality cotton or linen. These are both common, affordable fabrics that come in a variety of weaves and colours. Due to their (often) tighter weaves, these fabrics usually have less stretch, making them ideal for embroidery. One hundred percent cotton or a cotton-blend fabric is a good choice for an embroidery base, particularly if you're stitching permanent hoop artworks. You can find these fabrics at most fabric or craft stores, but I often reach for Kona Cotton or Essex Linen by the Robert Kaufman brand. You're more than welcome to thrift fabric, tea towels, or clothing to stitch on as well, just pay special attention to the details I mentioned above: stretchability, opaqueness, and weave.

I'll also note that felt is a good base for embroidery, but a bit harder to stretch in a hoop and even harder to remove the hoop lines from afterward.

Nonetheless, it's a great material if you're looking to embroider ornaments or stocking designs.

A last note when choosing a fabric is to pay special attention to the colour you're selecting with the design. A white or cream base is my typical go-to, but from time to time my artistic background gets the better of me and I experiment with a coloured fabric. It really does wonders for allowing lighter colours to pop (see the Holiday Rocking Horse project in particular), or even just to complement the colours already in the pattern (see Festive Joy and Bows and Baubles). I know coloured fabric can be a bit more intimidating, but when looking at the embroidery as a whole artwork, playing with colour can completely alter the finished piece. I will note that darker fabrics are a bit harder to transfer a pattern to (unless you're using a water-soluble adhesive pattern), but I'll explain this further in the Pattern Transferring Methods section.

Shopping List

USE THIS SHOPPING LIST when you're sourcing and collecting your supplies to get started on your embroidery projects! You can find most of these items at your local craft and fabric shops, but don't be afraid to search out independent fibre arts websites or Etsy shops online, too. You can also go thrifting for unique embroidery tools like antique scissors or vintage fabric, and interesting bases like napkins, tea towels, or aprons.

- DMC embroidery floss (in required colours)
- Wood or plastic embroidery hoops (4 inch (10 cm); 5 inch (13 cm); 6 inch (15 cm); and 7 inch (18 cm))
- Embroidery needles (size 5 or a multipack)
- Needle threader (optional)
- Needle minder (optional)
- Thimble (optional)
- Embroidery scissors
- All-purpose/craft scissors
- Fabric scissors (optional)
- Pinking shears (optional)
- Transfer pens or pencil (recommended: FriXion heat erasable pen)
- Fabric (recommended: linen, 100% cotton, cotton-linen blend) or project base of choice (napkins, tea towels, clothing, apron)
- Fabric backing of choice (felt, cardboard)
- Water-soluble stabilizer (optional) (recommended: Sulky Sticky Fabri-Solvy stabilizer or DMC Magic Paper)
- Hair dryer/iron
- Wooden frame or stand (for displaying a finished project)

PATTERN TRANSFERRING METHODS

One of my most frequently asked questions about embroidery is "How do I get the pattern template transferred to the fabric?" It's actually a lot easier than you'd think! The following section will walk you through two common methods for transferring the pattern templates in this book onto your project base. I've also included a bonus transfer method that is handy for stitching on clothing or darker fabric.

You can find the pattern templates in the very back of the book, where you can cut them from the binding and use them for transferring. You can also print out the patterns at rockynook.com/handmade-holiday/.

Just remember that your transferred pattern doesn't need to come out perfect. As you can see from my transferred patterns (**FIGURE 1.2**), some lines are a bit shaky, altered, and redrawn. So long as you stitch neatly and make sure to cover these lines or use heat erasable ink, you'll be golden!

Once you've secured your fabric of choice in your hoop, flip it over so you're looking at the back side of the fabric showing in the inner hoop. This angle will allow you to place the front of the fabric flush with the pattern template when transferring it. Then place your hoop with the front side of the fabric over the top of the pattern, trying to center the pattern template in the hoop. From here you can use you're decided transferring method to trace the pattern.

The key to being able to see the pattern template through the fabric is using a light source, as in the following two methods.

1.2

Method One: Daylight Transfer Technique

For method one, you'll use a windowpane as your light source (**FIGURE 1.3**). Take the single pattern page you'd like to transfer and sandwich it underneath your stretched fabric hoop so the daylight shines through the page and the fabric. You may need to fold the other book pages back a bit to lay the page flat against the window. Or you can remove the pattern transfer page with scissors for easier use.

Using your decided pattern transferring tool, trace the pattern starting from the top left and working your way down or around clockwise. This will keep you from smudging any transfer lines if you're using a pen. If you're left-handed, start from the top right and work your way down or around counterclockwise.

Method Two: Light Table/Tablet Transfer Technique

For method two, you'll use a lit-up light table or tablet as your light source (**FIGURE 1.4**). For a light table this is pretty straightforward—just turn the table on and proceed. For a tablet or iPad, I've found using a screenshot or a downloaded image of a white background works well. Use the guided access feature to lock and stabilize the page to keep the screen from glitching or moving around while tracing. You can also use the top screen of a laptop in a pinch, just be gentle when tracing.

Using your decided pattern transferring tool, trace the pattern starting from the top of the left and work your way down or around clockwise. This will keep you from smudging any transfer lines if you're using a pen. If you're left-handed, start from the top right and work your way down or around counterclockwise.

1.3 *You can utilize the sunlight from a window to trace your pattern.*

1.4 *Alternatively, you can use the light of a tablet to reveal your pattern for tracing.*

Speciality Method: Water-Soluble Adhesive Stabilizer

This bonus specialty method requires the use of a water-soluble stabilizer. I would recommend checking out the Sulky-brand Sticky Fabri-Solvy water-soluble stabilizer or DMC Magic Paper. The benefit of these adhesive stabilizers is that you can easily trace the designs from this book onto them, stick them on the fabric or clothing of your choice, and then wash away the template and stabilizer after you've finished stitching. This is an ideal method for working with dark fabric or on clothing that cannot easily be stretched in a hoop (**FIGURE 1.5**).

1.5 *This type of stabilizer dissolves in water and rinses away.*

For this specialty method, you'll want to use one of the two methods mentioned previously when tracing the pattern onto the stabilizer paper of your choice. Be sure to use a water-soluble pen that won't bleed when you wash the stabilizer away. Make sure to sandwich the pattern template paper between a light source and the stabilizer on top and trace away. Once your pattern is traced, you can cut down the remaining stabilizer around the template and place it on your fabric or clothing of choice. Now you're ready to get stitching! Once you're done, use warm running water and gently rub away the stabilizer around your work.

You can alternatively print your pattern templates on to the stabilizer paper of your choice. Just make sure your sheet is facing the correct way for the ink to print on the water-soluble side and use an ink that won't bleed (such as a laser jet).

PATTERN TRANSFERRING TOOLS:

- **Heat erasable pen:** This is my preferred and most recommended transfer tool, as you can transfer the pattern with clean and visible lines that are easy to erase with a hair dryer or iron after you're done stitching.

- **Basic lead pencil:** When I first started embroidering, I used a basic lead pencil to transfer my designs. This works well too, but be advised that the lines aren't removable, so be more diligent in covering them with your stitches (or use a light enough hand that they fade away naturally as you're working).

- **White gel pen or chalk pencil:** I would only recommend using a white pen or chalk pencil when working on a darker fabric, because they tend to leave visible marks that are hard to remove. In the case of darker fabric, you can use the specialty method of water-soluble adhesive paper, as described above.

Once you've finished tracing your pattern, double check that you haven't missed any parts of the image, unscrew your embroidery hoop, and remove the fabric from between the hoops. From here you'll place the transferred pattern fabric (with the pattern side up) and any additional pieces of fabric (underneath the pattern fabric) on top of the smaller inner hoop. Place the larger outer hoop over top of the pattern fabric and press down gently to fit the hoops together and sandwich the fabric between them.

Continue by lightly tightening the screw or bolt at the top of the hoop until it is closed (**FIGURE 1.6**). Before you tighten the hoop completely, make sure to center the orientation of the pattern and straighten out any bumps or wrinkles in the fabric. Finish off by fully tightening the hoop and you're ready to get stitching!

STARTING YOUR PROJECT

So—you've picked up this book full of festive holiday projects, have given it a good read through, collected your supplies, and now you're finally ready to get started! From setting up your hoop to threading your first needle to actually sitting down with a cup of cocoa and your brand-new project, this is the beginning of your new favourite pastime.

1.6 *The hoop keeps your fabric taut!*

Step One: Getting Your Project Base Ready

The first thing you'll need to do is get your chosen fabric or project base in the hoop and ready for stitching. If you're planning on stitching a pattern in a hoop as a permanent artwork, that means cutting out the squares of fabric for your hoop. My general rule for cutting out an ideal-sized square is to leave an additional 2" around the edges of your hoop when cutting (e.g., for a 4" hoop, cut out a 6" × 6" square of fabric).

If you are planning on using two layered squares of fabric to create a more opaque background, cut two squares of the same size. You can use normal craft scissors or fabric shears to do this, but if you want to go a step further, use pinking shears to cut a zig-zag edge to keep the fabric from fraying.

If you're planning on embroidering an alternative project base like a napkin, tea towel, or apron, wash and iron out the item to get it ready for step two.

Step Two: Transferring Your Pattern Template

Once you've gotten your fabric or project base ready for stitching, the next step is to transfer your selected project pattern. Using your desired transfer method and transfer tools (see page 12), load your hoop and transfer your template design. I'll mention this again in the project sections, but each template has a black outline and grey directional lines to use while stitching. You can trace the directional lines if you'd like or simply make little directional ticks when tracing as a reminder.

Now that your pattern is transferred, make sure to flip the fabric over so the template is facing up. Make sure your pattern is oriented properly and your hoop is tightened adequately before stitching. Remember, you'll want the surface to feel taut like a drum!

Step Three: Cutting and Separating Your Embroidery Floss

Now that your project is all set up, you'll need to get your other primary tool ready to stitch: the embroidery floss. This starts off with determining how many strands you'll need for your first stitches. Most bundles of embroidery floss will consist of six strands of thread making up one piece of floss. For most of the patterns in this book, you'll be using three strands far more than the full six strands, so you'll need to separate them each time you're starting a new colour of working thread.

Cut about half an arm's length (approximately 60 cm) of floss. If you're brand new to embroidery, you can cut a shorter strand of about a foot (30 cm) to make working with the floss a bit easier. Separate the floss by gently pulling the threads apart, with three threads on each side. If this is proving to be a challenge, you can also take out one thread at a time and put them back together in two pairs of three.

Step Four: Knotting Your Floss and Threading Your Needle

Now that you've got your project all ready, the last setup step is tying your floss into a secure knot and threading your needle. Tie a small knot at the end of your floss, leaving a 1 to 2 cm tail. I find with three strands of floss it's better to double knot your working strand so it's more secure (it may take a couple of tries to get the knots to line up). You can also work with the one knot, just be gentle when pulling the first strand through the fabric so you don't end up pulling the knot out the other side.

Next, take the opposite end of the floss and thread it through the needle's eye. You can use a needle threader if you've secured one, but I find threading three strands through a size 5 needle to be fairly easy by just wetting the tip and pushing it through. From here you're ready to put all these tools to use and get stitching!

Step Five: Start Stitching

To start the stitching process, pull your needle up through the back of your working fabric or project base and start your first stitch with the required stitching technique. In the case of most patterns, you'll start with the most delicate line details or greenery first, as they will build out a base for your project. I'll always leave raised details like French knots and woven wheels until the end because they are easy to snag while stitching.

Each pattern in the project section will have instructions that will detail how to go about the stitching process, but every embroidery artist is different, so feel free to stitch the patterns in whichever order you prefer. You can also see page 61 for more information about layering stitches.

Step Six: Ending Your Working Thread

As you're stitching, you'll get to the end of your working thread and need to start a new one. This will become second nature after a while. When you've reached the end of your working thread, secure it so it doesn't come loose as you continue stitching. This is especially important if you're working on a project like a napkin, towel, or piece of clothing where the back side will see a bit more wear and tear.

Secure these threads by winding your needle under an existing strand at the back of your project (**FIGURE 1.7A**), looping it around again (**FIGURE 1.7B**), and through the loop to secure a knot (**FIGURE 1.7C**). From here you can pull any remaining floss through a few more strands and

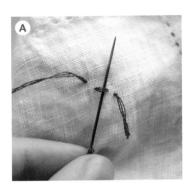
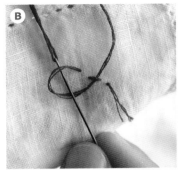
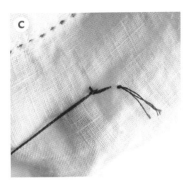

1.7

snip it close to your project. This is important so you're not catching and tangling any loose threads at the back of your hoop as you're stitching. Alternatively, you can split your strands in half and tie the two groups together to make an easy knot. Don't forget to trim your ends afterward, just make sure to snip them quite short so they don't catch and pull.

Step Seven: Taking Breaks While Stitching

One of the other crucial steps while stitching is taking breaks! I often find myself spending hours upon hours sitting in bed or on the couch and stitching away while binge watching my favorite show. But as my mom loves to remind me, it's important to stop for a little while every now and again. Make sure to get up and stretch your hands, stretch your legs, and, especially, give your eyes a break. Don't get me wrong, embroidery is a peaceful and relaxing activity, but it does take a good deal of time so be conscious of pacing yourself while you're creating some handmade magic.

Step Eight: Finishing Your Project

If you're planning of keeping your project as a permanent hoop artwork, you can see Finishing Your Hoop Art (page 21) to read about how to finish your hoop. If you used a heat erasable pen, you'll also want to pull out your hair dryer or iron to remove any remaining marks.

There are also additional steps you can take to polish off your finished project, including adding a felt back to your hoops, or an iron-on permanent interfacing patch to cover any stitches on a tea towel, napkin, or piece of clothing. It's totally okay to also leave your stitches uncovered! Chances are you won't see the back of the stitches often and embroidery is a fairly sturdy art form if you've done a good job at pulling your stitches securely and knotting off all your working threads. It's also personal preference, but I like having my stitches show to remind myself of all the hard work and time that went into crafting my artwork.

Step Nine: Be Proud of Yourself and Marvel at Your Finished Creation

You've done such a wonderful job at practicing patience, thoughtfulness, and commitment in working through your project. Take the time to appreciate your creation, sign the back of the hoop if it's a permanent artwork, and make sure to wrap it with care if you're gifting it to a loved one. No matter how you feel about your finished piece, remember that, like all art forms, building a skillset takes time and practice. So be proud of what you've accomplished and get ready to start your next project!

TROUBLESHOOTING

You'll more than likely run into a few knots and tangles as you're stitching, so I've detailed a few tips and tricks on how to avoid and deal with these snags while you're working!

Embroidery Floss Tangles

Embroidery floss is bound to tangle from time to time, especially if you're working with a longer strand. The easiest way to resolve this issue is to use shorter strands of floss, but if you'd rather use a longer strand, use three instead of six strands, and take the time to run your fingers down the length of floss to smooth it out. From time to time you may have to pull the strands through the best you can and start a new piece of floss if it's being extra bothersome.

Some embroidery artists will also use a thread gloss to help keep the strands together while stitching. Metallic floss is especially notorious for tangling easily, so in this case I'd recommend a thread gloss or simply using a single thread from the six-stranded floss when you'd like to add an extra sparkle to your work.

If you find your thread is tangling while pulling it from its DMC floss bundle, try pulling it down from the end with the numbered floss band. Taking the additional step to wind your floss around embroidery bobbins will save you from having to deal with piles of tangled floss in the future!

Surprise Knots

Sometimes you'll be on a role stitching only to pull your needle through and find it won't budge. You turn your fabric over and find an unwanted knot! Most of the time unpicking these knots is as simple as gently wiggling your needle inside it to loosen the knot and pull it free. However, if the knot has been pulled too tight, it may be easier to literally "cut your losses" (or in this case your floss) and start fresh. Make sure to still tie off your working strand the best you can to keep the remaining floss secure. Then you can cut off your floss past the knot and move forward with a new working strand.

Loose Threads Pulled Through from the Back

From time to time you'll be working on stitching flower petals with a purple floss only to have a mysterious green strand come up as you're pulling your floss through. This is often because the pesky green thread has been caught by your needle and brought to the front. One way to counteract this is to keep your finished strands tied off and neatly cut at the back of your hoop. In the case that the strands get caught anyway, you can resolve it by locating the loose thread at the back and gently pulling it back into place (at the back of the hoop) with your needle.

Wrinkles and Puckering

One of the most bothersome things that embroidery artists deal with is wrinkles and puckering of the fabric while they are stitching. This can be counteracted by ironing your fabric prior to putting it in the hoop, but more often it has more to do with the stretchability and tension of your fabric, as well as the quality and grip of your hoop. By using fabrics with a tighter weave and less stretch, and hoops that hold the fabric tightly, you should be able to maintain a fairly tight and wrinkle-free surface.

If you're stitching and your fabric starts to pucker, even after you've made sure to start with a good fabric base, it could be that you're pulling your stitches too tight, or that you need to readjust your fabric tension and re-tighten your hoop. If you're determined to stitch on a fabric that has more stretch to it, you can also use an iron-on stabilizer to add more stability to your fabric and help to counteract puckering when you remove the hoop.

Tearing out Unwanted Floss/Stitching

Sometimes when you're having an off day while stitching, or you've just used a colour you're not quite happy with, or you've just pulled a French knot too tightly and now it's just a tiny dot, you'll need to take your handy embroidery scissors and cut out your work. For satin stitches, snip carefully across your work and then use your needle to pull out the stitches at the back. For multiple French knots, it can be easier to snip them at the front and start fresh, or pull them out carefully rather than cutting your floss at all. For woven wheels, it's easier to cut the middle spokes at the back of your hoop and pull out your work from the front. Some people might be inclined to use a thread seam ripper, but as embroidery is delicate, you'll need to be careful you don't catch other stitches or tear the fabric as you remove other parts.

Removing the "Hoop Ring"

Because the tension and tightness of your hoop is so crucial to a good stitching base, the side effect is that sometimes when you remove the fabric from your hoop, it can leave a prominent "hoop ring" or "hoop burn" on the fabric. Luckily, this can be remedied by ironing, steaming, or washing your item. You can also limit "hoop burn" by removing the hoop from any non-permanent embroidered bases (like napkins, tea towels, or clothing) to give the fabric a tension break when you're not actively working on your project.

Washing Embroidery

Embroidery is actually a pretty sturdy art form that can take gentle washing easily. But beware that once you've washed the floss, it might shift the way the strands lie and give it a different look then your freshly stitched piece. If you end up using a different brand of floss then DMC, also be careful when washing garments of a lighter colour in case the dye in the floss bleeds.

Red Fibres Latching onto White Threads

As embroidery is a fibre art form, it's bound to have fibres and smaller threads that latch onto others as you're working. This is especially true of bright vibrant colours like red latching onto (and being very visible against) lighter colours like white. I've had this particular issue when working on my Candy Cane Blooms pattern (page 111) and it usually causes the red fibres latching on to give the white floss a pinkish hue. It's easily avoided by stitching with the lighter shades first, followed by the darker, more vibrant shades. This is true of other darker shades like blue, black, and brown, too. By being mindful of the way you're stitching with your colours, you'll keep your white or lighter floss shades clean and unaltered.

Stitching at Night Mishaps

It's common for people to work on their embroidery projects at night, especially after a day of work when you want to wind down—particularly during the fall and winter months when the sun goes down earlier. My advice is to get cozy and work away, just be careful to double check the colours you are using (warmer lamp light will often change the look of whites, yellows, greens, and browns) and use adequate light so you can see where and what you're stitching. Book lights are really good for this, so you can still stitch by the fire or the magic of Christmas tree lights.

FINISHING YOUR HOOP ARTWORK

Once you've pulled the finishing stitches through, tied off your final knot, and marvelled at your handmade creation, you'll probably wonder how you're going to finish off your project. The good news is, it's actually a simple process! I'll cover two different methods for finishing your project as a finished hoop artwork, in addition to some bonus touches to polish off the back of your hoop and how to finish loose embroidery projects.

Method One: A Floss Closure

1. Carefully trim your fabric about an inch and a half (4 cm) in a circle around your hoop with either fabric scissors or sharp craft scissors (**FIGURE 1.8**).

2. Knot your floss and bring your needle up from the underside of the fabric near the top of the hoop (**FIGURE 1.9**).

3. Wind your needle back down a half inch away from the first stitch (**FIGURES 1.10A–B**).

4. Continue by working your needle up and down around the hoop fabric clockwise. Once you get back to your first stitch, pull the working floss gently but firmly to tighten the closure (**FIGURES 1.11A–B**).

5. Loop your needle once around the last stitch and knot it closed by running your needle through the loop. Do this a few times to really secure the closure and snip off your floss (**FIGURES 1. 12A–B**).

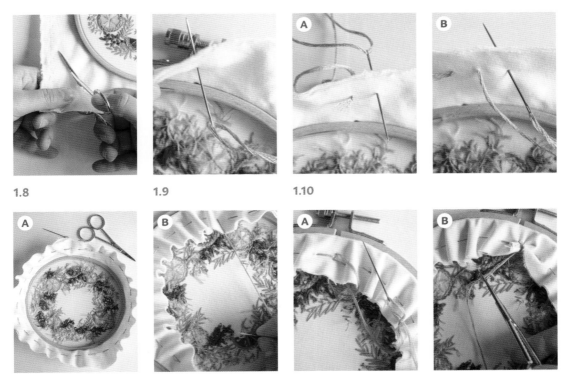

1.8

1.9

1.10

1.11

1.12

Method Two: A Double-Sided Tape Closure

1. Carefully trim your fabric about an inch (2.5 cm) in a circle around your hoop with either fabric scissors or sharp craft scissors (**FIGURE 1.13**).

2. Using the same scissors, make cuts on your loose fabric inward to create one-inch (2.5 cm) strips. For smaller hoops, you can cut smaller strips if you wish (**FIGURE 1.14**).

3. Cut small strips of double-sided tape about an inch long by the depth of your hoop wide (usually about 1 cm) and place it on the inner wood hoop (**FIGURE 1.15**).

4. Take the fabric strips below the tape and carefully press them in toward the center of the hoop and down onto the tape (**FIGURE 1.16**).

5. Continue with steps three and four, working your way clockwise around the hoop until you've fully closed the fabric (**FIGURE 1.17**).

Bonus Finishing Touches: Covering Your Hoop Back with Fabric, Felt, or Cardboard
If you've decided to stitch one of the project patterns on a base such as a napkin, tea towel, or piece of clothing, you might want to finish the back of the project by covering the stitching work and loose threads. You can do this with fabric stabilizer patches or squares of iron-on interfacing. Alternately, you can leave the back

1.13

1.14

1.15

1.16

1.17

1.18

uncovered, just make sure all of your strands are neatly tied off and cut short to keep them from snagging while using and washing the projects.

It's completely personal preference, but some embroidery artists like to finish the back of their hoops with special backing (**FIGURE 1.18**). You can do the same by using a piece of fabric, felt, or a cardboard circle to cover your backing threads. You can even go as far as using patterned scrapbooking paper, personalized stamps, or a name and date card to further personalize how you finish your hoop.

PROJECT INSPIRATIONS

After you've flipped through the pattern projects in this book and decided on the one to make, the next decision is deciding what fabric you'll embroider the design on. Stitching the project in the hoop as a finished artwork is perfectly fine, but if you'd like to go a step further, use these designs on other items, too!

Re-framed Artworks

The great thing about stitching embroidery in a wooden or plastic hoop is that it acts as an easy frame. But you can purposefully cut your fabric in a bigger square and reframe it in a specialty hoop, or even stretch the fabric over a rectangular frame and display it in a classic photography frame. Find some DIY fabric stretching videos and get crafty! Just make sure to pre-plan the size of your fabric and be gentle with your finished product so it doesn't get damaged during framing (**FIGURE 1.19**).

Ends of Scarves

Most of the smaller patterns (and even some of the larger ones) would be great for embroidering on the ends of scarves. You just need to pay

attention to the width of the scarf (for placement of the pattern) in addition to the fabric thickness, weave, and stretchability.

Sweaters

Another idea is to use a smaller pattern (in the corner) or a larger pattern (in the center) of a sweater! As previously mentioned, make sure to pay attention to the fabric thickness, weave, and stretchability of the sweater you're working on. Most sweaters have a bit more stretch to them, but you can use an iron-on stabilizer on the back of the fabric (in the place you plan to stitch) to give you a sturdier base. Simply add a stabilizer square large enough to cover your project's surface area, and trim away the excess stabilizer after releasing the sweater from its hoop.

1.19

Tea Towels

All of the pattern projects in this book would make excellent additions to tea towels (**FIGURE 1.20**). Be mindful of the thickness, weave, and stretchability of the fabric you'll be embroidering (see page 9), and make sure you place that pattern in such a way that it will be centered even when the towel is folded.

Napkin Corners

There are a few particular patterns in this book that are more ideal for napkins (**FIGURE 1.21**), mostly those that are 4" and 5" hoop sizes. Some of my pattern suggestions for napkins include Poinsanta Hat, Cup of Christmas, Festive Joy, and Scarves and Snowflakes. Be mindful of the fabric thickness, weave, and stretchability of the fabric you'll be embroidering and make sure you center your pattern on the napkin corner both folded and unfolded.

1.20

Linen and Canvas Bags

Another lovely idea is to use these patterns to embellish linen or canvas drawstring bags and totes. They'll make beautiful handmade vessels for gifting presents like other handmade items or festive goods like chocolate coins and Christmas oranges.

Stockings

A last inspiration idea is to consider using these patterns to decorate Christmas stockings. You'll need to pay attention to the size and width of the stocking, as it will determine your ability to stretch it in a hoop for stitching and the ease of working on the pattern. As always, be mindful of the fabric thickness, weave, and stretchability. Cotton, linen, and felt stockings will work well for stitching on.

1.21

CHAPTER 2

Stitch Library

NOW THAT YOU'RE A LITTLE MORE FAMILIAR with the basics of embroidery and have had a moment to flip through the patterns, it's time to familiarize yourself with the basic stitches you'll need to get stitching! Whether you're a pro with embroidery floss or just beginning to learn the art form, my hope is that the following section of the book will give you a good understanding of some workhorse embroidery stitches.

FESTIVE STITCH SAMPLER

I designed the festive stitch sampler (on the next page) to correlate with the Stitch Library so you can practice the stitches you'll need for the patterns found later in this book. The stitch library is ordered according to the instructions for the sampler so you can move easily from step to step. It's a great initial project for beginner embroidery artists, or if you just want to sharpen up your stitching skills. I used five Christmas-y colours so that you might hang your stitch sampler as a piece of abstract Christmas décor, but you can also stitch the sampler with one or two shades of your choice.

You'll want to get your stitch sampler pattern transferred as normal (this will give any new stitchers a chance to practice transferring) and then work your way through the Stitch Library with your sampler in hand. If you're an experienced embroiderer and would rather forgo the sampler, simply use the Stitch Library as a reference for the basic stitches you'll need as you work on the project of your choice!

STITCH GUIDE

A 3866, back stitch, 3 strands

B 3866 and 777, whipped back stitch, 3 strands

C 777, chain stitch, 3 strands

D 3866 and 3052, satin stitch, 3 strands and lazy daisy loops, 6 strands

E 3866, satin stitch, 3 strands

F 3866 and 326, satin stitch and turkey work pom-pom, 3 strands

G 3866 and 777, wavy petal stitch, 3 strands and cross knots, 6 strands

H 988, lazy daisy branch, 6 strands

I 3052, satin leaf stitch, 3 strands

J 3052, chain stitch, 6 strands

K 326, satin stitch, 3 strands

L 988 and 777, holly leaf stitch, 3 strands and French knots, 6 strands

M 3052 and 988, herringbone leaf stitch, 3 strands

N 777, 3-spoke woven wheel rose, 6 strands

O 326, 5-spoke woven wheel rose, 6 strands

P 3866, long back stitch, lazy daisy loops, and French knots, 6 strands

MATERIALS

- 7" Square of Fabric
  (I used Kona Cotton in the shade White)
- Embroidery Floss
  (see colour guide for suggested hues)
- Embroidery Hoop (5" or 12 cm)
- Embroidery Snips/Scissors
- Pattern Transferring Tools + Transfer Method of Choice
- Size 5 Embroidery Needle

COLOUR GUIDE

○ 3866

● 326

● 777

● 3052

● 988

Back Stitch

This is a workhorse stitch that you'll use often while embroidering line work. It's a useful stitch for outlining shapes and words, in addition to creating stems for leaves and flowers.

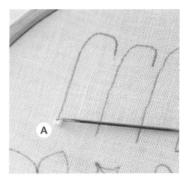

1. Knot your thread and bring it up through the back of the fabric (**A**).

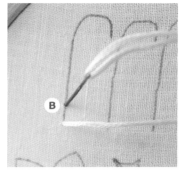

2. Insert your needle approximately a cm away from where you first pulled the thread through (**B**).

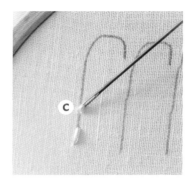

3. Pull the thread through to the back and then bring your needle to the front of the fabric another cm away (**C**).

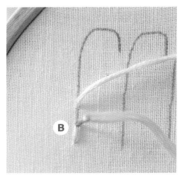

4. Insert the needle back through the previous hole (**B**) and pull through so the string is taught.

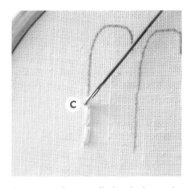

5. Insert the needle back through the fabric toward the front at point **C**.

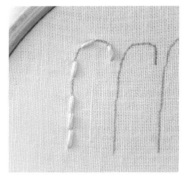

6. Repeat Steps 1 through 4 until you've reached the desired length of your line and then tie off your thread at the back.

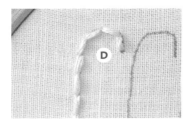

Alternatively, you can stitch all your alternating stitches first to the desired end of your line (**D**), then circle back to finish off the remaining gaps (you'll need to work backward). Make sure to tie off your thread at the back.

In the stitch sampler, you can use the back stitch method to start the second cane.

Whipped Back Stitch

The whipped back stitch is a back stitch with a twisted effect. It's perfect for stems, outlines, and a clean and textured look when stitching words. It's also really handy for stitching easy candy canes.

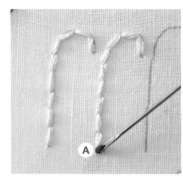

1. Start by stitching your desired line with a basic back stitch, making each stitch at about a cm (the size of a pinkie).

2. Bring your red floss and needle up near the base of your candy cane (**A**).

3. Bring your needle underneath the first stitch from one direction and gently pull through (**B**).

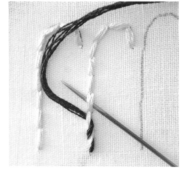

4. Bring your needle up to the next stitch, and underneath again from the same direction (**C**).

5. Continue bringing your needle underneath each stitch from the right side until you've reached the end of your back-stitched line.

6. Finish your whipped back stitch by tying off the thread in the back.

TIP for Whipped Back Stitching. I've found that whipped back stitches always come together smoother when you bring your needle under the stitches from the right. This means you may need to turn your work as you're stitching. If you stitch with your left hand, try stitching the back-stitched portion upside down so you're still technically coming from the "right" side.

If you decide to use a metallic floss for a back stitch (such as in the Rainbow Snow Globe Pattern), my recommendation is to only use one piece of thread for the back stitch and one piece for the whipping.

Chain Stitch

The chain stitch creates a line of chained loops perfect for outlining. It's also useful for creating a knitted look (hats, scarves) and bushy greenery (garlands, wreaths).

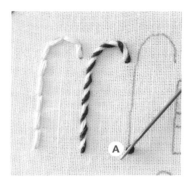
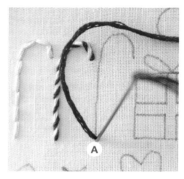

1. Knot your thread and bring it up through the back of the fabric (**A**).

2. Bring your needle back down through the same hole. Avoid catching your original knot (**A**).

3. Pull the thread until you have a small loop, but don't pull the loop through all the way (**B**).

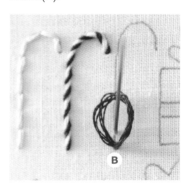
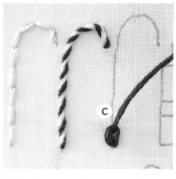
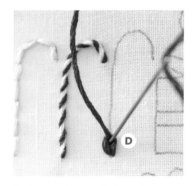

4. Bring the needle up through the back of the fabric in the middle of the loop (**B**).

5. Pull your needle in the direction you want your loop to sit until it pulls into a snug chain (**C**).

6. Insert the needle back into the previous hole (**D**), being careful not to pull the loop all the way through.

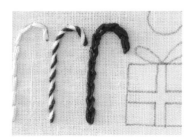

7. Repeat steps 2 through 5 until you've reached your desired length of stitches and tie your thread off at the back.

TIP **for Chain Stitch.** If you run out of floss while chain stitching, treat the stitch like a lazy daisy stitch (see page 37). Bring your next working thread up through your previous loop to cover the finishing knot and keep chain stitching.

Satin Stitch

The satin stitch is another workhorse stitch that is often used to fill in shapes and blocks of colour. You'll find it used quite a bit throughout the patterns in this book in many different ways. Beginner and expert embroidery artists alike struggle with satin stitches, so over the next few pages you'll find a few different methods for creating this stitch. There are also examples of using this stitch to make basic shapes like circles, hearts, and triangles. I always use three strands of floss when satin stitching, as it yields a smoother surface.

Satin Stitch: Method One

The first method of satin stitching is the one I use most often, as it allows for the best use of a single piece of floss and leaves a clean backing. The only downside is that this method is a bit more challenging to master because you're bringing up the stitches so close together. It takes a bit of practice but is a handy method when you're using a good deal of satin stitch in a pattern and want to stretch your floss.

A bonus tip for this method is to make sure you don't pull your stitches too tight, as it will bunch up your satin stitching and keep it from lying flat.

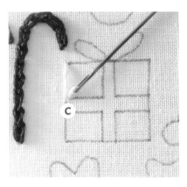

1. Separate your threads into three strands, knot your thread, and bring it up through the back of the fabric (**A**).

2. Insert your needle into the fabric at the width you wish your satin stitch to be (**B**). For other shapes, insert your needle in the center from top to bottom.

3. Bring your needle up through the back next to the edge of your first stitch, being careful to leave a tiny gap between both holes (**C**).

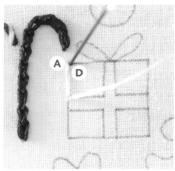

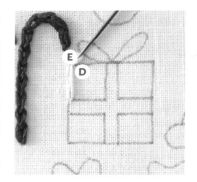

4. Insert your needle right next to the side of the linear stitch (**A**), being careful to leave a tiny gap between both holes (**D**).

5. Bring your needle up through the back next to the edge of your last stitch (**D**), being careful to leave a tiny gap between both holes (**E**).

6. Repeat steps 2 through 5, being careful to keep the threads straight and pulled flat to the fabric. Make sure not to pull the thread too tightly to prevent the fabric from bunching. Tie off your thread in the back.

Satin Stitch: Method Two

This second method uses a bit more thread, but it provides a more secure satin stitch base. This is the satin stitch technique I would recommend for beginners! Changing where you bring up your needle will result in a bulkier but more stable backing (see step 6 as an example).

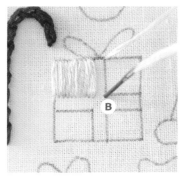

1. Separate your threads into three strands, knot your thread, and bring it up through the back of the fabric (**A**).

2. Insert your needle at the width you wish your satin stitch to be (**B**). For other shapes, insert your needle in the center from top to bottom.

3. Bring your needle up through the back next to the top stitch (**A**), being careful to leave a tiny gap between both holes (**C**).

continued . . .

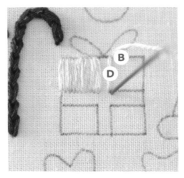

4. Insert your needle next to the bottom stitch (**B**), being careful to leave a tiny gap between both holes (**D**).

5. Repeat Steps 1 through 4 until you've reached the desired length of your stitching, and then tie off your thread at the back.

6. Run your needle through one of the floss strands and tie off a knot to finish your satin stitch.

Satin Stitch: Method Three

The third method is a combination of methods one and two. It works by creating a base of separated lines that are then filled in to finish the satin stitch. This is a good way to practice method one, while also providing a more solid base by separating the first lines. Just be careful to still place your stitches relatively close together.

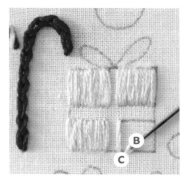

1. Separate your threads into three strands, knot your thread, and bring it up through the back of the fabric (**A**).

2. Insert your needle the width you wish your satin stitch to be (**B**). For other shapes, insert your needle in the center from top to bottom.

3. Bring your needle up through the back next to the edge of your first stitch (**B**), being careful to leave a full line gap between both holes (**C**).

4. Insert your needle a stitch length away at the top, next to (**A**), being careful to leave a tiny gap between both holes (**D**).

5. Bring your needle back up through the top right (**E**) another vertical stitch length away.

Continue steps 1 through 4, making sure to leave a vertical stitch length between each line and alternating from the top and bottom.

6. Once you've reached the end of your shape, loop back and fill in the remaining gaps.

7. Finish off the satin stitch square and tie off your thread in the back.

8. Finish off the last square of the present on the stitch sampler with whichever satin stitch method you prefer.

Long-Distance Satin Stitch

Some projects require a longer satin stitch, like the ribbon on the stitch sampler gift. You can use whichever satin stitch method you would like to practice the long-distance version of the satin stitch.

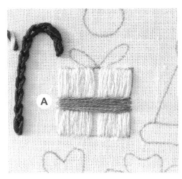
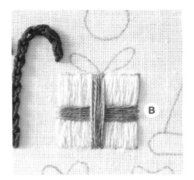

1. Separate into three strands, knot your thread, and bring it up through the back of the fabric (**A**). Use whichever method you'd like to fill in the horizontal section of the ribbon.

2. Knot your thread and bring it up through the back of the fabric (**B**). Use whichever method you'd like to fill in the vertical section of the ribbon.

3. Tie off your satin stitch and use your needle to run down the strands and straighten them out until you're happy with the ribbons.

Satin Stitching a Circle

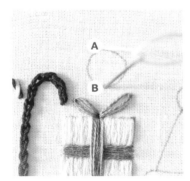

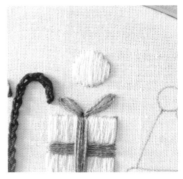

1. Use three strands, knot your thread, and bring it up through the back of the fabric at the top of your circle (**A**) and down the center to the bottom (**B**).

2. Use your preferred method of Satin Stitch to fill in the first half of the circle, being careful to line up your stitches with the circular shape.

3. Continue by filling in the other half of the circle with the same satin stitching method. Stitching the circle this way will keep your two sides balanced.

Lazy Daisy (Detached Chain Stitch)

The lazy daisy stitch (also known as the detached chain stitch) creates a single loop perfect for stitching bows or other looped details. Later on, you'll also find a lazy daisy branch (multiple lazy daisy loops to create easy branches).

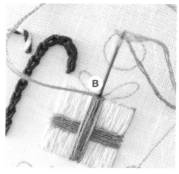

1. Knot your thread and bring it up through the back of the fabric at the bottom of your loop (**A**).

2. Bring your needle back down through the same hole. Avoid your original knot (**B**).

3. Pull the thread until you have a small loop, then bring your needle up through the middle of the loop (**C**).

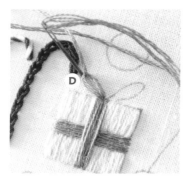

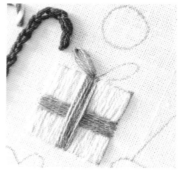

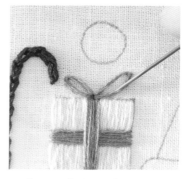

4. Pull gently to tighten your loop around the needle, then bring the needle up and tuck it behind the top of your loop (**D**).

5. Pull your needle down to secure the loop and then tie it off at the back; or continue stitching your other lazy daisy loops.

6. If you pulled your loop too tightly, use your needle to gently reshape the loop until you're happy with its curve and shape.

Why Is It Called a Lazy Daisy Stitch?

The lazy daisy stitch is so named because embroidery artists use the detached loops to create "lazy" flower petals. You'll find the lazy daisy stitch used in this book for leaves on loopy branches and mini wreaths.

Satin Stitching a Heart

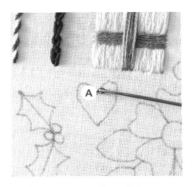

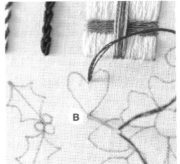

1. Separate your threads into three strands, knot your thread, and bring it up through the back of the fabric at the top of your heart (**A**).

2. Insert your needle down at the bottom tip of the heart (**B**).

3. Pull your needle down to create the first stitch down the center. This will create the center barrier for when you stitch both sides.

4. Use your preferred method of satin stitching to fill in the first half of the heart, being careful to line up your stitches with the curved shape.

5. Continue by filling in the other half of the heart with the same satin stitching method. Stitching the heart this way will keep your two sides balanced.

TIP for Satin Stitching Other Shapes like Stars. When satin stitching any kind of free-floating shape, my approach is always to start with a line down the center and work your way out on either side. For a star, you can work your way out to either side and up into the points. You can practice this in the Bows and Baubles pattern!

Satin Stitching a Triangle

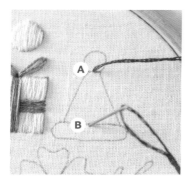

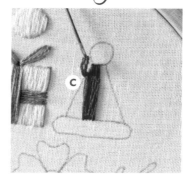

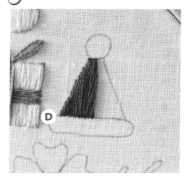

1. Separate your threads into three strands, knot your thread, and bring it up through the back of the fabric at the top of your triangular shape (**A**) and back down to the bottom of the center (**B**).

2. Use your preferred method of satin stitching to fill in the first half of the triangle, being careful to line up your stitches with the sharp shape (**C**).

3. Continue stitching down the left side, shortening your stitches until you reach the bottom tip (**D**).

4. Continue on the other side of the triangle, being careful to keep your sides even.

TIP for Satin Stitching Triangles. Keeping a straight edge on a satin triangle can be a bit tricky and it takes some practice to line up your stitches properly. Method two of satin stitching is easier because you can bring your stitches closer together without them pulling.

Satin Stitching an Oval

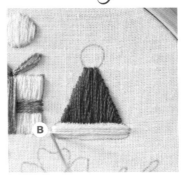

1. Knot your thread and bring it up through the back of the fabric at the right middle of your oval (**A**).

2. Bring your needle across to (**B**) and continue stitching, working up and down on either side to keep your satin stitching even.

3. Continue stitching on the bottom half with your preferred method to fill in the lower half of the oval (**C**).

4. Finish off your oval shape by using your chosen method to fill in the top of the oval. Tie off your work at the back and use your needle to comb the lines straight.

Turkey Work Pom-Pom

This section details how to use a pinned-down loop called a "turkey work" stitch to create a fluffy pom-pom effect. The trick to successful turkey work is to keep your pinned-down loops as close to each other as you can, so when you trim them, you'll have a full and bushy pom-pom. This will serve you well whenever you'd like to stitch a hat pom-pom like in the Merry Mittens pattern. These would also make great alternates for flower centers!

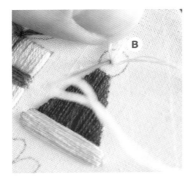

1. Knot your thread and bring it up through the back of the fabric at the center of your circle outline (**A**).

2. Bring your needle back down to create a small loop and pin it down with your thumb (**B**).

3. Bring your needle up from the right of the center of the loop (**C**) and back over the center and down to the left (**D**).

4. Pull your needle down to secure a tiny knot over the center of the loop to secure it in place. Push up your loops when stitching around your center loop so you can see where you are stitching your next loops.

5. Continue adding these secured loops around your initial loop to fill in the whole circular shape, making sure to turn so your loops face in all directions out from the center.

6. Once you've completely filled in your circular outline, you'll take a pair of sharp embroidery scissors and gently cut down the loops to create the fluffy pom-pom.

Lazy Daisy Branch

The lazy daisy stitch is a workhorse stitch that's great for creating easy petals and leaves. For this part of the stitch sampler, you'll practice how to stitch multiple lazy daisies on a whipped back stitch to create a basic leafy branch. This will come in handy later, especially for the Citrus and Berries pattern!

1. Start your branch by filling in the middle line with a three-stranded whipped back stitch.

2. Bring your needle up at the base of the first loop (**A**).

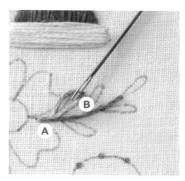

3. Create a small loop. Bring your needle down at the same base (**A**) and then back up again inside the loop (**B**).

4. Pull your needle down gently to secure your first loop. Use your needle to shape your loop until you're happy with it (**C**).

5. Continue by alternating with the next closest loop on each side of the branch until you've stitched in all the loops.

6. Fill in the other lazy daisy branch on the stitch sampler, and you're ready to move on to your next stitch.

Covered Satin Leaf Stitch

The satin leaf stitch is another essential stitch for filling in any leaf or pointed flower shapes. The stitch sampler features two different methods: the covered leaf, which is often found up against flower petals and under roses, and the extended leaf, which often extends out from blooms. Both use the same starting method (a stitch down the center of the leaf) but have different techniques from there.

1. Separate your six-strand floss into three strands. Knot your thread and bring it up through the back of the fabric (**A**).

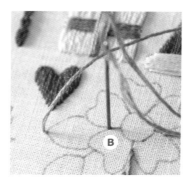

2. Bring your needle down the center line to the base of the leaf nearest your flower's outer edge (**B**).

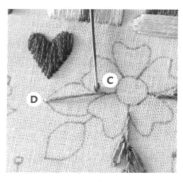

3. Bring your needle up again to the right of the bottom stitch (**C**) and back down next to the top of your initial stitch (**D**).

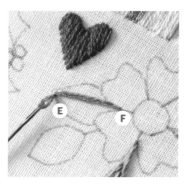

4. Bring your needle up again on the other side of your initial stitch (**E**) and back down at the base of your leaf again (**F**).

5. Continue by alternating between steps 3 and 4, until you've filled out the shape of your leaf!

Extended Satin Leaf Stitch

The extended satin leaf stitch features the basic satin leaf stitch with an extended branch. You can use this method to fill in any full leaf shape, whether it's attached to a flower or simply free floating!

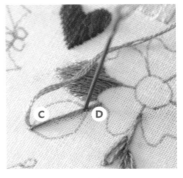

1. Stitch in your branch with a three-stranded back stitch, then bring your needle up at the top of the leaf (**A**).

2. Bring your needle down the center line to the base of your branch (**B**).

3. Bring your needle up again to the right of the top stitch (**C**) and down again at the bottom of the leaf (**D**).

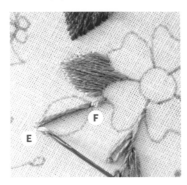

4. Bring your needle up again on the other side of your initial stitch (**E**) and back down at the base of your leaf again (**F**).

5. Continue by alternating between steps 3 and 4, until you've filled out the shape of your leaf!

Wavy Petal Stitch

You can use the wavy petal stitch to fill in petals with a curved edge, using a specialized satin stitching method. This section will go into depth on how to use longer and shorter stitches when satin stitching for a smoother and rounder appearance without crowding the base of the petal. You'll find this helpful for wavy petals found in the Feathers and Florals and Stuffed Stocking patterns.

1. Knot your thread and bring the needle up through the back of the fabric at the top of the petal (**A**).

2. Bring your needle down in the middle of the petal to the center (**B**).

3. Bring your needle back up to the right of your initial top stitch, being careful to not catch the initial knot (**C**).

4. Pull the needle down alongside your middle line and insert it just slightly above your bottom stitch (**D**).

5. Continue stitching to the left of the initial lines but make sure to bring your needle slightly up again before inserting it to create a triangle shape (**E**).

6. Repeat step 5, but bring your stitch slightly higher again to create a triangle shape (**F**).

Bring your needle up again near your last stitch (**G**).

continued . . .

7. Bring the stitch down to the center of the petal to tie your triangle stitches together and mesh the satin shape (**H**).

8. At this point you should be close enough to the edge of the petal to finish it with a few more stitches all the way to the center to round out the shape.

9. Once you've rounded out one half of the petal, you can bring your needle back up to the left of the center line and repeat steps 3 through 9.

10. Finish off the petal and run your needle along the strands to smooth down the satin stitch toward the center. From here, fill in the other petals around the flower.

11. Tie off your work at the back, and you'll be ready to fill in the center with your chosen method.

Cross Knot Stitch

The cross knot stitch is exactly what it sounds like: a simple knot created by crossing one tiny stitch over another to create a round little knot. You can also achieve a simple knot without crossing them; the crossing just gives it more depth. These are ideal for filling in flower centers and adding dotted textures. This stitch will serve you well in the Pretty Poinsettia and Poinsanta Hat patterns.

1. Knot your thread and bring it up through the back of the fabric at the outer edge of the flower center (**A**).

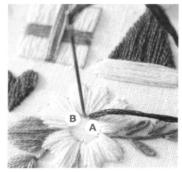

2. Bring your needle down just one needle tip width below (**A**) and insert it back into the fabric (**B**).

3. Pull the thread down gently to create a small knot. If you'd rather finish the knot here instead of crossing it, you can simply skip to step 7.

4. Bring your needle up through the back of the fabric above the initial knot in between **A**, **B**, and **C**.

5. Insert the needle back down below the initial knot, being careful to keep your needle as close to it as you can to keep your knot tight (**D**).

6. From here you'll pull the thread down gently to finish your knot. It takes a bit of practice to line it up properly.

continued ...

7. Use your new cross stitch technique to fill in the outer edge of the flower's center.

8. Repeat and fill in another row of circular stitches around the last circle. If you're unhappy with your stitches, now is the time to unpick them or cut them out and start again.

9. Fill in the remaining open center with cross knots. Tie off your work and you're ready to move on to the next stitch!

Chain Stitch Garland and Wreath

Now that you've learned the chain stitch, you can put it to good use in crafting mini wreaths, strung garlands, and even mitten cords. This method will be useful in the Merry Mittens, Stuffed Stocking, and Christmas Cabin patterns. For this part of the stitch sampler, you'll practice using the chain stitch in a circular method to create a mini wreath.

1. Knot your thread and bring it up through the back of the fabric through one of the dots (**A**).

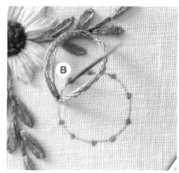

2. Create a loop and bring your needle up through it at the next closest dot (**B**).

3. Gently pull your loop taught and repeat step 2 to work your way around the circle.

4. Once you've made your way back to the initial loop, bring your needle right near your starting loop (**C**).

5. Pull your needle down inside your initial loop to attach the chain together (**D**).

6. Once you've finished your wreath, tie off your work and use the tip of your needle to shape the loops. From here you can add cross knots or French knots over the top as berries, if you'd like.

TIPS for Using the Chain Stitch as a Garland. Use the same curved chain-stitching method to fill in arched shapes to turn them into loopy foliage. This will come in handy when stitching the arched garlands on the roof of the Christmas Cabin pattern.

I stitch most of my greenery with six strands of floss for a fuller effect, but you can vary your threads for different looks.

Holly Leaf Stitch

The holly leaf stitch is a commonly used stitch during the holidays to make the signature shape of holly leaves. It is essentially a herringbone stitch following the curved leaves of the holly. As the holly berry is such an iconic Christmas motif, you'll find that it pops up in several of the patterns in this book! If you'd like to practice the herringbone leaf first, see page 54.

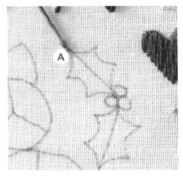

1. Separate your six-strand floss into three strands. Knot your thread and bring it up through the back of the fabric (**A**).

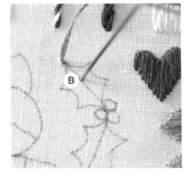

2. Bring your needle down the center line of the leaf a short length away from the top (about a third of the leaf) (**B**).

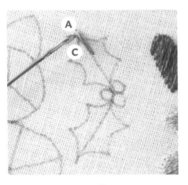

3. Bring your needle up again to the left of the first top stitch (**A**) along the top curved edge (**C**).

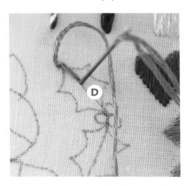

4. Bring your needle down and across, just below the bottom of your first stitch (**D**).

5. Bring your needle up on the other side of the top stitch (**A**) but this time, to the right (**E**).

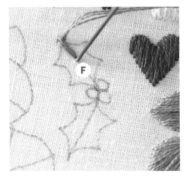

6. Bring your needle down again over the top and just below the middle stitch (**F**). The overlapping stitches will create the herringbone effect.

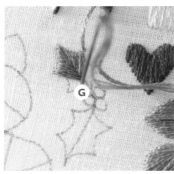

7. Repeat steps 3 through 6 to fill out the leaf. When you get close to the edge, you may need to shorten your stitches and overlap them slightly to fill in the narrower middle part (**G**).

8. Finish each tip edge by bringing your needle back down toward the center. Work your way down to the bottom of the leaf and finish with stitches toward the base.

9. Make sure to tie off your leaf and then continue the stitch sampler by adding in your French knot "holly berries."

French Knot & Faux French Knot

The French knot stitches can be a little frustrating at first, but once you get the hang of them, they can be handy workhorse stitches great for holly berries, fairy lights, fluffy mitten cuffs, and layers of snow. The trickiest part with French knots is being careful not to catch your knot as your needle pierces the fabric (also not pulling too tightly when securing your knots!). For this stitch, patience and practice make a world of difference. I've also included an easier "faux" French knot for beginners!

French Knot

1. Knot your thread and bring it up through the back of the fabric (**A**).

2. Wrap the thread around your needle twice and pull the leftover thread taught as you do so (**B**).

3. Keeping the wrapped thread pulled tight, push the tip of the needle down and back close to your original hole. Be careful not to catch your original knot (**C**).

4. Pull your needle down to pull the taught thread into the knot. This might take a bit of practice.

5. Fill in the rest of the knots, being careful not to pull your working thread too tight or you'll pull out the finished knot.

Faux French Knot

1. Knot your thread and bring it up through the inner edge of your circle (**A**) then down again right beside the first hole to create a loop (**B**).

2. Bring your needle up though the loop in the center of the circle (**C**).

3. Pull the thread taught until the loop pulls tight against the working thread (**D**).

4. Push the needle down behind the loop and as close to the original hole as possible (**E**).

5. Pull your needle down gently but firmly to create your faux knot. For a normal pattern, you can continue stitching the rest of the knots from here.

6. Continue the stitch sampler by filling in the last holly berry with the French knot method of your choice.

TIP **for French Knot.** French knots can be a bit of a confusing method to get right. You have to maintain tension on the wrapped thread so that when you pull your needle down and through it comes together nicely in a knot. Hold the end of the loose working thread between your fingertips closest to the wrapped parts and pull down your needle to maintain this tension.

Herringbone Leaf Stitch

The herringbone stitch is a fun way to make a leaf look intricate and detailed simply by alternating the side you're stitching from and crossing the strands to create the herringbone effect. This is a good method to variate from the satin leaf stitch and a great technique for stitching holly leaves (see page 50).

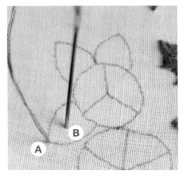

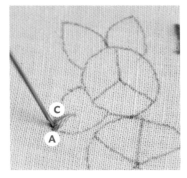

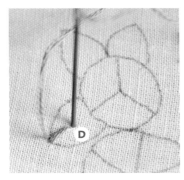

1. Bring your thread up through the back of the fabric (**A**). Bring your needle down the center line of the leaf a short length away from the top (about a third of the leaf) (**B**).

2. Bring your needle up again to the right of the first top stitch (**A**) along the top curved edge (**C**).

3. Bring your needle down across and just below the bottom of your first stitch (**D**).

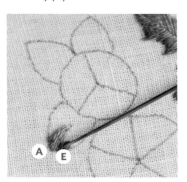

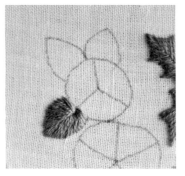

4. Repeat steps 3 through 4 on the right side, bringing your needle up by (**A**) and then down over the center line. Continue this method alternating on each side (**E**).

5. Continue the criss-crossing method down the curved edges of the leaf. Your bottom stitches may overlap a bit, but this is normal. Practice by filling in the other leaves with the same method and alternating colours.

TIP for Stitching the Herringbone Leaf. Make sure you're crossing your stitches overtop of each other a tiny bit as you bring each new stitch down to the center. Keep moving your stitches down as you go so they don't all get bunched in the middle.

Toward the bottom of your leaf, the stitches may overlap slightly as you run out of space. You can shorten your stitches slightly to avoid this (as exemplified in the wavy petal stitch on page 45) or simply overlap them slightly to finish the bottom of the leaf.

Three-Spoke Woven Wheel Rose

The woven wheel rose stitch is the perfect stitch for crafting (you guessed it) roses. I start mine the classic way with weaving the needle under and over "spokes" and then using an overlapping stitch method to give the rose a blooming finish. My patterns use three spokes and five spokes based on the size of the rose in question.

1. Knot your thread and bring it up through the back of the fabric in the center of the spokes (**A**).

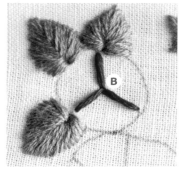

2. Stitch the three spokes with a simple back stitch (**B**).

3. Bring your thread up near the center (but not through the middle hole) between two of the straight stitches (**C**).

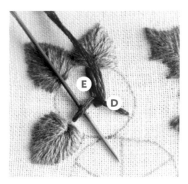

4. Working counterclockwise, loop your needle under the first spoke to the right (**D**) and under, over the next spoke (**E**).

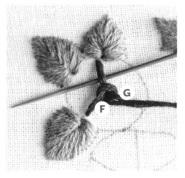

5. Continue weaving your needle under (**F**) and over (**G**) each alternating spoke around the wheel to build up the base of your rose.

6. You'll continue this weaving method until you fill half of the rose. Be careful not to pull the weaving too tight, or your center will bunch together.

continued . . .

7. Bring your needle up at the middle of your previous stitch to start the layering process (**H**).

8. Bring your needle down again around the edge of you rose center (**I**), about 2 cm away. Be careful to work gently so as to not pull your center.

9. Bring your needle up again in the outer middle of your last stitch (**J**), keeping your stitches close together.

10. Continue this overlapping method, working your way all around the rose. Fill up the remaining space left in your circle outline.

11. Once you've covered all of your spoke edges and filled out your circle, you can do a final round of overlapping stitches to cover any leaves.

12. Once you've finished all your overlapping stitches, carefully tie off your thread in the back and use your needle to carefully fluff and shape your rose petals.

Five-Spoke Woven Wheel Rose

1. Knot your thread and bring it up through the center of the five spokes.

2. Stitch the five spokes with a simple back stitch (**A**).

3. Bring your thread up near the center (but not through the middle hole) between two of the straight stitches (**B**).

4. Working counterclockwise, loop your needle under the first spoke (**C**) and over the following spoke (**D**).

5. Keep weaving under and over the spokes to fill in your rose's center. Keep your stitches fairly loose so your rose will be fluffy.

6. Once you've filled in half of the circular outline with your weaving, bring your needle up at the outer edge to start layering your stitches.

continued . . .

7. Continue working your way all around the rose with the overlapping stitches until you've filled up the outline.

8. Once you've covered all of your spoke edges and filled your circle, you can do a final round of overlapping stitches to cover any leaves.

9. Carefully tie off your thread in the back and use your needle to fluff and shape your rose petals.

10. If necessary, go back and add in any additional overlapping stitches to connect roses close by or to cover up where the rose covers the leaves.

A Unique Way to Stitch a Woven Rose:

The method above for stitching roses was adapted from the traditional stitch called a woven "wheel" stitch, in which you stitch your spokes and wind your needle under and over until you've completely filled your circular outline. The finishing result looks like the top of a rose, and thus became a good to stitch for creating this kind of flower in embroidery artworks.

When I stitched the roses this way, they ended up looking a bit too round. I wanted petals that framed the rose on the outside, giving the flower the illusion of blooming. By using overlapping stitches to frame out your rose, your final product is a much more realistic flower.

Long Stitch (Snowflakes)

Long stitches are essentially back stitches that stretch a greater length. You'll use long stitches for snowflakes, tree branches, and other long line details. When using long stitches, be careful with your stitch placement, so you're able to maintain good tension in your stitches. This will keep them from bunching or puckering.

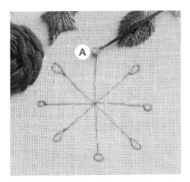

1. Knot your thread and bring it up through the back of the fabric (**A**).

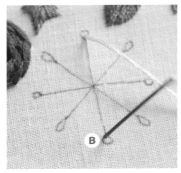

2. Insert your needle down at the end point of your line (**B**).

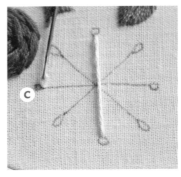

3. Bring your needle up to the left of the end of the stitch, directly crossing your first vertical line and pull through (**C**).

4. Bring your needle across and insert it down at the other end of your line (**D**).

5. Bring your needle up at the top edge of the diagonal line above your last stitch (**E**) and down across to the other end of the line (**F**).

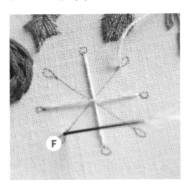

continued . . .

... Long Stitch (Snowflakes) continued

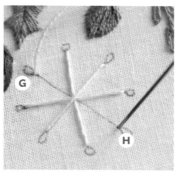

6. Bring your needle up at the top edge of the diagonal line above your last stitch (**G**) and down across to the other end of the line (**H**).

7. To complete the stitch sampler, use tiny lazy daisy stitches at the edges of the diagonal lines and French knots at the edge of the vertical and horizontal lines.

8. Make sure to tie off your working thread at the back of your hoop, being careful not to pull out your French knots!

Finish off the back of your stitch sampler by closing up the threads.

You've now practiced all the stitches you'll need to create the holiday patterns that follow!

LAYERING STITCHES

Layering a Whipped-Back Stitch Over a Satin Stitch

When you know there will be whipped-back-stitched elements over top of satin-stitched elements (such as in the Rainbow Snow Globe pattern), satin stitch around them so you can remember where to place your whipped-back stitches later. This also allows the whipped lines to sit properly against the satin stitch without disturbing it.

Simply be conscious of these lines as you're stitching the satin elements. Draw your satin stitches right up to, but not over, the lines. This will leave a faint outline of where your whipped back stitch will go later. One you've finished all of the other satin-stitch elements in your pattern, you can go back in with a back stitch followed by a whipped-back stitch. Make sure to whip your back stitches by bringing your needle under from the right and turning your work as you go.

Layering Tree Branches

The trick to layering tree branches for a more dimensional and realistic look is to start with the darkest shade and work out. This is because these darker base layers will act as the shadow layers and be covered with the lighter highlighted areas as you continue filling in the remaining branches. Continue with the remaining colours and finish with the lightest highlighting shade.

You'll also want to pay close attention to the direction your branches are stitched in to give the best effect. For the patterns in this book, following the grey directional lines will help to get you started, but when you're filling in the remaining space around your base layers, just be mindful that all your additional stitches all follow the direction of the prior stitches.

Layering Satin Stitches Close Together

The trick to layering satin stitches close together is to start with the inner satin-stitched elements and work your way out. This method works best because it allows you to bring your needle up in an open space and down against the edge of an already satin-stitched area. It'll keep you from bringing your needle up near the edge of other satin stitches and ensure that you're not disturbing work you've already stitched.

Layering Woven Roses Over Greenery

I love using woven roses in my patterns as they provide a fun bit of texture to any piece! The key to layering them the right way with leaves or stems, is to start with the greenery first and add in the roses over top. This works well as it allows you to stitch the greenery right up to the base of the rose and also makes layering the rose petals over the pre-stitched leaves a breeze.

CHAPTER 3

Projects

THE FOLLOWING PROJECTS SECTION OF THE BOOK features 16 Christmas-forward patterns that I designed and hand stitched. I hope you have the loveliest time stitching up these patterns and displaying them proudly or gifting them to your loved ones. There are a few things I want to note about the projects before you get started:

The following projects and patterns feature a whole rainbow of colours. All the colour palettes are noted using the DMC shade range, but please feel free to substitute the colours for any embroidery floss you have on hand. If you're picking up floss for several projects, make sure to cross reference your colour guides as many of the projects feature my same, go-to shades of certain colours.

All of the patterns at the back of the book have been sized to fit the hoop noted in the materials list. Make sure to center the template design within the center of your hoop when transferring it. The projects are featured from the smallest scale (4 inches) to the largest scale (8 inches) and vary in complexity.

Each pattern has a colour guide and a stitch guide that notes which colours, stitches, and how many strands of floss to use for each element. You'll want to use this information, along with the Stitch Library and Instructions, to work through each project.

I've included additional tips for each pattern to lend a helping hand, but sometimes it just takes a bit of trial and error to get a stitched element looking exactly how you want it to look. Don't be afraid to cut out your work and start over, and make sure to take plenty of stretching breaks while working. Remember to give yourself lots of grace and just have fun with the embroidering process!

Poinsanta Hat Pattern

WHEN I FIRST STARTED BRANCHING OUT from more traditional floral designs (and especially with Christmas patterns), my biggest challenge was how to fill in shapes without using only satin stitches. Although I now love satin stitches, in the beginning they felt daunting. Eventually, I got creative and started filling in larger subjects with smaller shapes like flowers instead. Thus, the Poinsanta Hat was dreamt up. You might have already guessed by the title, but this pattern features a bit of a twist on a traditional Santa hat as it's made up of Poinsettia flowers! To continue the whimsy vibe, it also features detached chain stitch petals to fill in the white band and pom-pom. Because of this, this pattern is quite beginner friendly and a fun project for any skill level. Alternatively, you can fill in the white band and pom-pom with a turkey work stitch for a fluffier effect!

MATERIALS

- 6" Square of Fabric (I used Essex Linen in the colour Bordeaux)
- Embroidery Floss (see colour guide for suggested hues)
- Embroidery Hoop (4" or 10 cm)
- Embroidery Snips/Scissors
- Pattern Transferring Tools + Transfer Method of Choice
- Size 5 Embroidery Needle

COLOUR GUIDE

- 321
- 777
- C816
- 471
- 3847
- Blanc

STITCH GUIDE

A 321 and 777, satin leaf stitch, 3 strands; 471, cross knot, 6 strands

B C816, satin leaf stitch, 3 strands; 3847, cross knot, 6 strands

C C816, satin leaf stitch, 3 strands

D Blanc, lazy daisy stitch, 6 strands

INSTRUCTIONS

1. Start by filling in the petals of the Poinsettia flowers with three strands of the red shades (321 and 777) and a satin leaf stitch, starting at the tip of the leaf and working outward (**A**).

2. Finish off the same flowers with 471 and six-stranded cross knots in the center of the flower. If you'd like more texture, you can also use a French knot (**A**)!

3. Continue filling in the remaining Poinsettia flowers by using three strands of C816 and a satin leaf stitch to fill out all the flower petals (**B**).

4. Finish off the same remaining flowers with 3847 and six-strand cross knots for the center (**B**). If you decided to use a French knot in step 2, continue with the same technique.

5. Finish off any remaining flower petals with three strands of C816 and satin leaf stitches (**C**).

6. Lastly, use six strands of Blanc and a lazy daisy stitch to fill in the bottom trim and top pom-pom of the hat (**D**).

Cup of Christmas

IS THERE ANYTHING MORE QUINTESSENTIALLY CHRISTMAS then a festive mug of hot cocoa with whipped cream? This was the inspiration for the Cup of Christmas pattern, which features a lovely little cup decked with holly berries, candy canes, and sugar cookies. It's a fairly beginner-friendly pattern—the biggest challenge is the satin stitch whip. I've included grey directional lines on the patterns to help guide you, and I would recommend using the second method of satin stitching (see page 33) to make the process extra smooth. This pattern would make a lovely addition to the pocket of an apron or the center of a tea towel! You can customize the colour of the mug and sprinkles as you see fit, and even fill in the mug with a satin stitch if you're feeling extra crafty!

MATERIALS

- 6" Square of Fabric (I used Kona Cotton in the colour Sand)
- Embroidery Floss (see colour guide for suggested hues)
- Embroidery Hoop (4" or 10 cm)
- Embroidery Snips/Scissors
- Pattern Transferring Tools + Transfer Method of Choice
- Size 5 Embroidery Needle

COLOUR GUIDE

- ○ Blanc
- ● 3864
- ● 304
- ● 815
- ● 3052

STITCH GUIDE

A Blanc, satin stitch, 3 strands

B 3864, whipped back stitch,
3 strands

C Blanc and 815, whipped back
stitch, 3 strands

D Blanc, satin stitch, 3 strands
(icing); 3864, back stitch,
6 strands (cookie); 304 and
3052, cross knot, 3 strands
(sprinkles)

E 3052, holly leaf stitch,
3 strands

F 304 and 815, satin stitch,
3 strands

INSTRUCTIONS

TIP **for Beginners:** If you would rather avoid
the amount of satin stitching required for the
whipped cream (or if it's just giving you trouble),
you can alternatively outline the whipped
cream template lines with a simple back stitch
or whipped back stitch and the same Blanc
floss shade.

1. Separate your Blanc floss into three strands
   and fill in the white whipped cream with a
   satin stitch from the lower-left side. Work your
   way up and down the curved bars until you
   reach the other side. You may need to knot off
   your floss and continue reloading your needle
   as you go (**A**).

TIP for Satin Stitching the Whipped Cream:
Once you've stitched your first satin stitch "bar" of whipped cream, bring your needle up at the far side and back down against the stitches you've just completed. This will ensure that your satin stitch bars stay close together and give the proper illusion of the whipped cream rivets.

2. Outline the mug body and handle with a whipped back stitch, using three strands of the light brown (3864) (**B**). Make sure to keep your initial back stitches close together for a cleaner outline when you whip them.

3. Fill in the candy canes with three strands of (Blanc) back stitch and whip the lines with the dark red (815). Make sure to keep your back stitches quite small so your candy cane has a good number of stripes (**C**).

4. Satin stitch the white icing in the stars with three strands of the white (Blanc). Outline the cookies with six strands of the brown (3864) and finish the cookies with three strands of the red (304) and green (3052). Use three-stranded cross-knots for sprinkles (**D**).

TIP for the Sprinkles: If you're finding the double cross knots too bulky, you can use two strands of floss instead of three or simply do one knot instead of several overlapping knots.

5. Fill in your holly leaves with the holly leaf stitch and three strands of the green (3052) (**E**).

6. Finish off your holly berries with both of the red shades (304, 815) with a three-strand satin stitch (**F**). If you look closely, you'll see I alternated with the shades to give the berries more depth. If you'd like to skip this, you can simply fill in the berries with a single red colour of your choice.

TIP for Holly Berries: For more texture, you can also use six strands and French knots to fill in the berries; just be sure they meet the edges of your leaves. You'll also want to leave this step for the end of the project so you don't catch your berries while stitching other elements.

Festive Joy

WHEN I WAS DRAFTING NEW PATTERNS FOR THIS BOOK, I was inspired to create a word that you often see and hear during the holiday season. I knew I wanted to craft the letters out of festive elements, and loved the idea of stitching the letter "O" into a wreath! I tried out designs for "Noel," "Jolly," and even "Ho Ho Ho," but I settled on "Joy." It's a word that encompasses the happiness that can be found during the holidays in spending time with loved ones, sharing thoughtful gifts, or simply laughing over silly moments. This pattern would work great on a sweater, apron, or tea towel (which is what I stitched this pattern on). I used a green linen fabric to contrast and complement the colours in the pattern, but this would also look great on a neutral fabric that would allow the colours to pop!

MATERIALS

- 7" Square of Fabric (I used a green linen towel, but Kona cotton in the shade Tarragon would also work)
- Embroidery Floss (see colour guide for suggested hues)
- Embroidery Hoop (5" or 13 cm)
- Embroidery Snips/Scissors
- Pattern Transferring Tools + Transfer Method of Choice
- Size 5 Embroidery Needle

COLOUR GUIDE

- 326
- 814
- 3045
- 3364
- 3346
- 987

STITCH GUIDE

A 3364, whipped back stitch, 3 strands (outline of J)

B 3346, holly leaf stitch, 3 strands; 814, French knots, 6 strands

C 3346 and 987, chain stitch, 6 strands (wreath); 814 and 326, French knots, 6 strands

D 3364, whipped back stitch, 3 strands (outline of Y); 3045, whipped back stitch, 3 strands; 326, 814, 3346, and 987, satin leaf stitch, 3 strands (light bulbs)

INSTRUCTIONS

1. Start the "J" by using three strands of the lightest green (3364) and a whipped back stitch to cover the entire outline of the letter (**A**).

    TIP **for Stitching Letters with a Whipped Back Stitch:** Because you're whipping the back stitches of letters that end in sharp corners, you may want to run your needle down at the corners and back up again to give a more defined edge! (Otherwise, the edges might curve in when you round the corners of the letters.)

2. Next, stitch the holly leaves with three strands of the warm green (3346) all over the letter (**B**). Make sure your leaves end right up against the berry outlines so they mesh well together. You can then fill in the French knot berries with the darker red (814), or you can save them until the very end so you don't risk catching and pulling out the berries as you continue stitching.

3. From here, chain stitch the wreath of the letter "O." Start with the warmer green shade (3346) and fill in the lazy daisy loops, skipping every other loop in between (**C**).

TIP for Stitching the Lazy Daisy Chain in the Wreath: The pattern calls for alternating stitches using both of the greens (3346, 987) to create an extra-dimensional-looking wreath, but if you'd rather, you can simply fill in the whole wreath with one green shade. The same can be said for the two shades of the red berries. If it's easier to just stick to one shade, do what feels best for you!

4. Next, fill in the remaining loops with the cooler green shade (987), making sure to keep your loops fairly close to those already there to give your wreath a full look (**C**)! You can add any additional loops as you see fit.

5. To finish off your wreath, add in tiny French knot berries using six strands of the two reds (326 and 814) (**C**). It'll be easiest to do this where you see any natural gaps between the loops.

6. Move on to the "Y" by stitching the outline with three strands of the same lightest green (3364) and a whipped back stitch (**D**). This may be a bit trickier with the light strands, but you'll want to stitch around and under those strand lines so they don't end up too bulky when you stitch the light strands over the top later.

7. Next, use three strands of the gold (3045) and the same whipped back stitch to fill in the light bulb strands (**D**)! You'll want to back stitch all the light strands first, then go back in and whip them from top to bottom and up again.

TIP for Stitching the Winding Light Strands on the Letter "Y": Start at the top left and work your way to the middle and down with back stitches. Then tie off your thread and start again in the middle, working your way up to the top right of the letter. Start back at the top left and repeat the same method when you're whipping your back stitches, making sure to come at them from the right side for the cleanest outline.

8. Use 3 strands of all of the colours (326, 814, 3346, and 987) and a satin leaf stitch to fill in the bulbs (**D**). Make sure to use the same gold shade (3045) to add a few whipped back stitches over the base of the light bulb to connect it to the light strand.

TIP for Stitching the Light Bulbs: You'll want to start with a stitch down the middle of each light bulb and work your way out on either side using the satin leaf stitch method to fill in the bulbs. Then go in with a few back stitches over the base of the bulb to connect it to the light strand.

9. If you left your French knot holly berries unfinished on the letter "J," go back now and finish them off! Erase any template lines if applicable and you're all done!

Scarves and Snowflakes

AS A CANADIAN GIRL BORN AND RAISED WITH COLD AND SNOWY WINTERS, I have fond memories of making quite a few snowmen in front of our house growing up. There is something so fun and festive about crafting the snowy figures, especially around the holidays! This embroidered version features my unique style and snowflakes to fill in the snow balls of the snowman's body. Although the colour palette features a few purples and pinks to make this design appropriate all winter long, you're more than welcome to customize the colours of the scarf and beanie (or "toque" as we call them in Canada) as you see fit! This little snowman would look great with a classic Santa hat and green scarf as well...

MATERIALS

- 7" Square of Fabric (I used a white linen napkin, but Kona cotton in the shade White would also work)
- Embroidery Floss (see colour guide for suggested hues)
- Embroidery Hoop (5" or 13 cm)
- Embroidery Snips/Scissors
- Pattern Transferring Tools + Transfer Method of Choice
- Size 5 Embroidery Needle

COLOUR GUIDE

- 27
- 762
- 3856
- 3354
- 3727
- 3350
- 3863
- 3371

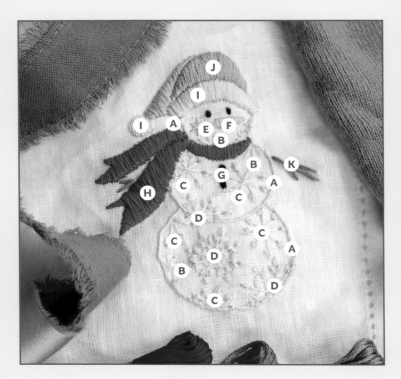

STITCH GUIDE

A 27, whipped back stitch, 3 strands

B 762, back stitch, 3 strands

C 27, back stitch and satin leaf stitch, 3 strands

D 762, back stitch and satin leaf stitch, 3 strands

E 3354, back stitch, 3 strands

F 3856, satin stitch, 3 strands

G 3371, satin stitch, 3 strands

H 3350, satin stitch, 3 strands

I 27, satin stitch, 3 strands

J 3727, satin stitch, 3 strands

K 3863, back stitch, 6 strands

INSTRUCTIONS

1. Start your snowman by stitching the snow-flakes with the light purple and grey (27 and 762) using three strands and a combination of back stitches, whipped back stitches, and satin leaf stitches (**A**–**D**).

   TIP for Stitching the Snowflakes: Start with the back-stitched bases of the snowflakes and add in the finer elements afterward. You can substitute the satin leaf edges with lazy daisy stitches or French knots if you'd prefer them! If you're stitching on a darker fabric, you can also substitute the entire body with the pure white DMC shade (Blanc).

2. Once you've stitched the snowflakes, finish off the borders of the snowman with the light purple (27) and a three-stranded whipped back stitch (**A**). Be careful to leave the border around the scarf and hat so that you can fill in the edges with satin stitches later.

3. Finish the remaining "blush" snowflakes on the snowman's cheeks with the light pink (3354) and a three-stranded back stitch (**E**).

4. Next, fill in the carrot nose with the light orange (3856) and a three-stranded satin stitch (**F**). Make sure to run your stitches vertically along the grey directional lines.

5. To finish your snowman's face, add the coal eyes with the dark brown (3371), using three strands and a satin stitch (**G**). While you're at it, fill in the buttons below with the same method!

    TIP **for Stitching the Coal Eyes:** Stitch down the center of the black template shapes and work out on either side to fill out the eyes. If your eyes look a bit "off" or too bulky, you can cut them out and try again with fewer strands (one or two).

6. Next, fill in the scarf with the magenta pink (3350) and a three-stranded satin stitch (**H**). Make sure to run your stitches vertically from the right edge of the scarf all the way across the neck and down to the bottom-left tip. You may need to shorten your stitches at the scarf points, but following the grey directional lines will also help.

7. Stitch the toque with a combination of the light purple (27) for the pom-pom (**I**), plus the mauve purple (3727) for the base of the hat (**J**). You'll want to use three strands of each colour and a satin stitch to fill in the beanie, following the grey directional lines.

    TIP **for Stitching the Beanie/Toque:** For the base of the hat, start with a stitch running down the center and work your way out with satin stitches on either side. When you start stitching the additional section of the hat draping down, begin at the top-right side and work your way down to the bottom where the hat connects with the pom-pom.

8. Finish your snowman by adding his stick arms around the scarf and body with a 6-stranded back stitch and the lighter brown (3863) (**K**).

Merry Mittens

THIS MERRY MITTENS DESIGN was inspired by the realization that I could use a simple chain stitch to replicate the look of a knitted beanie (or "toque," as we refer to them in Canada). After playing around with different knitted variations, I figured out that I could use the same method to fill in a pair of mittens! There's something so cozy and fitting about winter accessories leading up to the holidays. This pattern adds an extra festive touch with some holly berries and mistletoe, and makes for the perfect winter artwork to hang or gift during the holidays. You can change up the colours as you see fit and add in as many snowflakes as your heart desires!

MATERIALS

- 7" Square of Fabric (I used Kona cotton in the shade White)
- Embroidery Floss (see colour guide for suggested hues)
- Embroidery Hoop (5" or 13 cm)
- Embroidery Snips/Scissors
- Pattern Transferring Tools + Transfer Method of Choice
- Size 5 Embroidery Needle

COLOUR GUIDE

- Blanc
- 762
- Ecru
- 471
- 937
- 520
- 326
- 3747

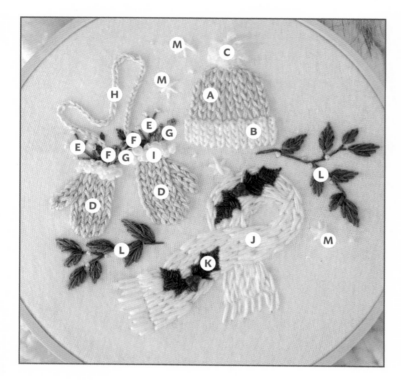

STITCH GUIDE

A Ecru, chain stitch, 6 strands

B Blanc, chain stitch, 6 strands

C Blanc, turkey work pom-pom, 6 strands

D 3747, chain stitch, 6 strands

E 937 and Ecru, back stitch, 3 strands and French knots, 3 strands

F 520 and 326: back stitch, 3 strands; satin leaf stitch, 3 strands; French knots, 3 strands

G 471, back stitch, 3 strands and lazy daisy stitch, 3 strands

H 762, chain stitch, 3 strands

I Blanc, French knots, 6 strands

J Blanc, back stitch, 6 strands

K 520 and 326, herringbone leaf stitch, 3 strands and French knots, 6 strands

L 937 and Ecru: whipped back stitch, 3 strands; satin leaf stitch, 3 strands; French knots, 6 strands

M Blanc, back stitch and cross knots, 6 strands

INSTRUCTIONS

1. Start the pattern by stitching the beanie using the white and tan shades (Blanc, Ecru) and a six-stranded chain stitch to fill in the knitted base of the hat (**A**, **B**).

TIP for Stitching the Beanie: Start by chain stitching the black center directional lines of the beanie from the top middle to the bottom edges. Continue with the same method on either side. Make sure to not stitch the outline of the beanie—as it will bulk out your hat shape too much. Repeat the same method with the cuff of the beanie.

2. Next, finish off your beanie by stitching the pom-pom with six strands of the white (Blanc) and a turkey work stitch (**C**). Use the grey directional dots in the circle as loop markers and fill in the circle as full of loops as you can!

3. After you've finished stitching the loops, take a pair of sharp scissors and carefully trim down the loops to create the fluffy pom-pom. You can start with some basic cutting to get the loops down to size and then go in again to shape your circle. Make sure to use your fingers to gently fluff up the shape as you're cutting.

4. Next, use the same 6-stranded chain-stitching method (that was used for the beanie) to fill in the mittens (**D**) with lavender (3747). Be sure to leave the white cuffs of the mittens open.

   TIP **for Stitching the Mittens:** Start by chain stitching the black center directional lines of the mittens from the top middle to the bottom edges. Continue with the same method on either side and make sure not to stitch the outlines of the mittens—as this will bulk out your mitten shapes too much.

5. Fill in the greenery sprouting out of the top of the mittens with the various suggested colours and stitches (**E–G**). Make sure you're splitting your floss where required so your greenery remains delicate enough to all fit in the space.

6. Finish off your mittens by using three strands of the light grey (762) and a chain stitch to stitch over the mitten's connecting line (**H**). Use six strands of the white (Blanc) and French knots to fill in the cuffs of the mittens (**I**). Start in the center and work your way out to create the fluffy cuffs. Alternatively, you can fill in the cuffs with a 3-stranded satin stitch and the same white shade.

7. Next, stitch the scarf with six strands of the white (Blanc) and a basic back stitch (**J**). Be sure to leave the holly berries and leaves open so you can fill them in later overtop of the scarf stitches. Make sure to use the same six strands to fill in the fringe of your scarf, too.

   TIP **for Stitching the Scarf:** Start at the bottom-left edge of the inner scarf (not the fringe) and start filling in the grey lines with a back stitch to create the texture of the scarf. Continue filling in these lines, working your way up the scarf and moving to the right. Make sure to work around the holly berry outlines and add in any additional back stitches as you see fit to create an opaque filling for the scarf.

8. Finish off your scarf by filling in the holly berries. Use three strands of the dark green (520) for the herringbone leaves and six strands of the bright red (326) for the French knot berries (**K**). Once you've filled them in, you can go in with additional white (Blanc) back stitches to fill in any gaps around the holly berries.

9. Lastly, fill in the mistletoe branches using the warm-green shade (937) with a three-stranded whipped back stitch (for the stems) and satin leaf stitches (for the leaves). Finish off these branches with six-stranded French knots in the cream shade (Ecru) (**L**).

10. To tie the whole design together, use six strands of the white shade (Blanc) to stitch the snowflakes (**M**). You'll use a combination of back stitches and cross knot stitches to fill in the snowflakes and snowy dots. Feel free to add in more around the design as you see fit or use the grey shade (762) if you want them to stand out more against the white fabric.

Starry Stockings

IS THERE ANYTHING MORE CLASSICALLY CHRISTMAS than stockings hung up by the tree? Growing up we had red, green, and gold stockings with teddy bears on the bottom edges. I've always loved pulling ours out year after year, and once I began designing embroidery patterns, it was on the top of my list to do some kind of pattern involving the iconic Christmas socks. This one is a classic take with five stockings of varying festive designs hung on a pine branch. Add in a few stars and you've got yourself a Starry Stockings pattern! This design would look so lovely on the pocket of some linen pajamas or across an apron front. It would look equally lovely on a cozy mantle or amongst a specially curated gallery wall. Feel free to alter the stocking colours as you see fit and maybe add some extra fun embellishments like gold thread or beads to really make your stockings sparkle!

MATERIALS

- 7" Square of Fabric (I used Kona cotton in the shade Natural)
- Embroidery Floss (see colour guide for suggested hues)
- Embroidery Hoop (5" or 13 cm)
- Embroidery Snips/Scissors
- Pattern Transferring Tools + Transfer Method of Choice
- Size 5 Embroidery Needle

COLOUR GUIDE

- 3865
- 3866
- C738
- 3864
- 801
- 3023
- 3362
- 936
- 934
- 814

STITCH GUIDE

A 801, whipped back stitch, 6 strands

B 3362 and 936, back stitch, 3 strands

C 3866, 3023, and 814: satin stitch, 3 strands; back stitch, 3 strands; lazy daisy stitch, 3 strands

D 3865, 3864, 3362, and 814: satin stitch, 3 strands; holly leaf stitch, 3 strands; French knots, 6 strands; lazy daisy stitch, 3 strands

E 3023, 814, and 934, satin stitch, 3 strands and lazy daisy stitch, 3 strands

F 3865, 814, and 3023: lazy daisy stitch, 3 strands; satin stitch, 3 strands; whipped back stitch, 3 strands

G 3866, 3864, and 814, satin stitch, 3 strands and lazy daisy, 3 strands

H C738, back stitch, 3 strands

INSTRUCTIONS

1. Start the pattern by stitching the base of the branch with six strands of the brown shade (801) and a whipped back stitch technique (**A**). Begin your back stitches from the right side and down the first branch, making sure to tie off your ends and restart your back stitch at the next point along the branch. Back stitch until you've reached the end of the whole branch on the left and follow the same pattern when whipping your back stitches.

2. Next, go in with the two green shades (3362, 936) and a three-stranded back stitch to fill in the pine needle branches (**B**).

TIP for Stitching the Pine Branches: Starting from the base of each branch, work your way around the branch, stitching with alternating greens. This will be easiest by starting with one green shade and going back in to fill in the needle gaps with the other shade. This will save you from constantly having to change colours.

3. Start with the "stitched" stocking on the far left and fill in the base with a three-stranded satin stitch in the cool white (3866). Continue by satin stitching the corners and top band with three strands of the lighter green (3023) and finish by back stitching around the border of the stocking with three strands of the red shade (814). Finish off the top loop of the stocking with 3 strands of the red (814) and a lazy daisy stitch (**C**).

   TIP **for Stitching the "Stitched" Stocking:** Start with the satin stitch first (for the base, top, and the bottom curved edges) and then go in after with a backstitch to add the "stitching" border details on top.

4. Next, stitch the base of the "holly berry" stocking with a three-stranded satin stitch using the warm white (3865) and the cool tan (3864). Make sure to stitch around the holly leaves and berries and don't forget to stitch in the tan lazy daisy loop at the top. Then fill in the holly leaves with a three-stranded holly leaf stitch using the green shade (3362), and the holly berries with six-stranded French knots using the red shade (814). Finish off the top loop of the stocking with three strands of the cool tan (3864) and a lazy daisy stitch (**D**).

5. Next up is the "striped" stocking! Satin stitch the stripes in the middle with three strands of both the green shade (934) and the red shade (814). Finish the stocking by using a satin stitch and lazy daisy loop with three strands of the lighter green shade (3023) to fill in the corners and top band of the stocking. Finish the top loop of the stocking with a lazy daisy stitch (**E**).

   TIP **for Stitching the Striped Stocking:** Start with the green shade first and satin stitch the lines running diagonally, then continue by filling in the remaining stripes with the red.

6. Stitch the fourth "knitted" stocking, starting at the bottom-right corner of the stocking (but above the red curved tip). Work your way up from the center line first with three strands of the warm white (3865). Continue stitching outward on either side from there, but don't stitch the stocking outlines as they will bulk up your stocking shape too much. Finish the remaining satin stitch and whipped back stitched details on the corners and top of the stocking with the green shade (3023) and the red shade (814). Finish the top loop of the stocking with three strands of the green (3023) and a lazy daisy stitch (**F**).

   TIP **for Chain Stitching the "Knitted" Stocking:** Run your stitches along the black lines of the stocking and curve them with the lines. You'll have to stop and start some of your chain stitches to go around the curved corners of the stocking details.

7. Lastly, stitch the "heart" stocking. Start by satin stitching the background of the stocking first with three strands of the cool tan shade (3864), making sure to stitch around the heart outlines (**G**). Then fill in the heart shapes with three strands of the red (814) and the satin-stitch method specifically for hearts. Finish the stocking by using a satin stitch and lazy daisy loop with three strands of the cool white shade (3866) to fill in the corners and top band, and finish the top loop of the stocking with a lazy daisy stitch.

8. Wrap up this pattern by stitching the stars! Use three strands of the sparkly gold shade (C738,) which is a special kind of floss with metallic shimmer in it, to back stitch the stars around the stockings (**H**). Make sure to pull the stitches of your stars gently to keep your fabric from bunching.

Bells and Beads

THIS PATTERN WAS INSPIRED BY THE SOFT NEUTRAL COLOURS and traditional elements of a Scandinavian Christmas mixed with a cozy cottage-core aesthetic. Featuring pine branches, brass bells, pastel ornaments, and pinecones, this pattern has all the cozy charm and simplicity of a quiet Christmas with your loved ones. Bells and Beads would be a great pattern to add to a cream linen apron or stocking to complement its simple and pretty motifs. It features a good deal of satin stitching, but it's a lovely pattern to work on bit by bit during cozy winter evenings by the fireplace or Christmas tree.

MATERIALS

- 7" Square of Fabric (I used Kona cotton in the shade White)
- Embroidery Floss (see colour guide for suggested hues)
- Embroidery Hoop (5" or 13 cm)
- Embroidery Snips/Scissors
- Pattern Transferring Tools + Transfer Method of Choice
- Size 5 Embroidery Needle

COLOUR GUIDE

○ 3866		● 3859	
● 842		● 3032	
● 3862		● 3051	
● 839		● 437	

STITCH GUIDE

A 3862 and 3051, whipped back stitch, 3 strands (branches) and back stitch, 3 strands (pine needles)

B 3866 and 842, chain stitch, 3 strands and lazy daisy stitch, 3 strands

C 3862 and 842, satin stitch, 3 strands and back stitch, 3 strands

D 3032 and 842, satin stitch, 3 strands and whipped back stitch, 3 strands

E 3859, 3866, and 842, satin stitch, 3 strands and whipped back stitch, 3 strands

F 842 and 3862, satin stitch, 3 strands (house, door, and windows) and back stitch, 3 strands (roof shadow line)

G 3862 and 839, satin stitch, 3 strands

H 437, 3032, and 842, whipped back stitch, 3 strands and satin stitch, 3 strands

I 3866 and 3051: satin stitch, 3 strands; back stitch, 3 strands; lazy daisy stitch, 3 strands (bow on present)

INSTRUCTIONS

1. Start the pattern by stitching the branches with three strands of the brown shade (3862) and a whipped back stitch, and three strands of the green shade (3051) with a back stitch for the pine needles (**A**).

2. Next, stitch the "knitted" stocking. Start at the bottom-right corner of the stocking (above the tan curved tip) and work your way up from the center line, first with three strands of the cool white (3866). Continue stitching outward on either side from there, but don't stitch the stocking outlines, as they will bulk up your stocking shape too much. Finish the remaining corners and top band with a six-stranded chain stitch and the brown shade (842). Don't forget to finish the top loop with six strands of the same brown shade (842) and a lazy daisy stitch (**B**).

3. Stitch the wooden beads with a three-stranded back stitch and the dark brown shade (3862) in addition to the satin-stitched beads with the lighter brown shade (842) (**C**).

TIP **for Stitching the Wooden Beads:** Just like stitching the satin circles in the Stitch Library, you'll want to start with a stitch down the middle and work your way out on either side. You can also add additional stitches overtop to perfect your circular shape and give your beads a nice, raised texture.

4. Next, stitch the star ornament detail with a satin stitch and three strands of the green shade (3032) in addition to a whipped back stitch and the light brown shade (842) for the ornament's looped twine (**D**).

5. From here you can use the same method to stitch the heart ornament! You'll use three strands of the pastel red shade (3859) to satin stitch the heart and three strands of the cool white (3866) with a three-stranded whipped back stitch for the heart's connecting loop. Use three strands of the light brown shade (842) with a whipped back stitch for the ornament's looped twine (**E**).

6. Next, stitch the little wooden cabin by using three strands of the brown shade (842) to satin stitch the house around the windows and door. This will be easiest to do by starting with a satin stitch down the middle and working your way out on either side. Follow the grey directional lines of the house and do your best to run your stitches right up to the window outlines and straight down through the gaps around them. Finish off the house by filling in the windows and doors with the dark brown (3862) with a three-stranded satin stitch, in addition to running a three-stranded back stitch under the roof lines to define it (**F**).

TIP **for Stitching the Cabin:** Start by satin stitching the base cabin and use the satin-stitched roof to cover the top edges of your satin-stitch. If your bottom stitches are uneven, you can run a single back-stitched line of the same medium brown shade (3862) to clean them up.

7. Move over to the pinecone and fill it in with a satin stitch using the two brown shades (3862, 839) with a three-stranded satin stitch. Fill in the lighter brown (3862) curved cones with a satin stitch starting with a stitch down the middle, and then continuing out on either side. You may need to really shorten your stitches to get to the edges. Use the same three-stranded satin stitching method to fill in the shadows with the dark brown (839) (**G**).

8. You'll then satin stitch the bell ornament. Use three strands of the gold colour (437) to satin stitch the base of the bell with a stitch right down the middle and then working your way out on either side. Use the same method for stitching the top gold loop and small circle of the bell. Once you've done the gold parts, you can use the lighter green (3032) to fill in the inside of the bell, but this time with a horizontal satin stitch. Finish the ornament with the light brown (842) and a whipped back stitch for the ornament's looped twine (**H**).

9. To finish off the Bells and Beads pattern, stitch the wrapped present. Use three strands of the cool white (3866) and a three-stranded satin stitch to fill in the base of the present. Finish by using the dark green (3051) along with three-stranded back stitching and lazy daisy stitches for the present's tied strings (**I**).

TIP **for Stitching the Present:** Follow the grey directional lines to give the satin stitch dimension and visible lines in between the edges.

Holiday Rocking Horse

THE INSPIRATION FOR THIS PATTERN came from all of the nostalgic childhood toys that dotted the Christmas storybooks. I had a lot of fun sketching up my own version of a white rocking horse decked out in poinsettias, stars, and holly berries. This pattern features a good bit of satin stitching, but I've done my best to make it fairly stitching friendly with the grey directional lines on the pattern template. This pattern would make a beautiful addition to any stocking or tea towel, not to mention the perfect handmade artwork on a styled holiday shelf!

MATERIALS

- 7" Square of Fabric (I used Kona cotton in the shade Rich Red)
- Embroidery Floss (see colour guide for suggested hues)
- Embroidery Hoop (5" or 13 cm)
- Embroidery Snips/Scissors
- Pattern Transferring Tools + Transfer Method of Choice
- Size 5 Embroidery Needle

COLOUR GUIDE

- 3033
- 739
- 3828
- 3831
- 815
- 3347
- 320
- 319
- 938

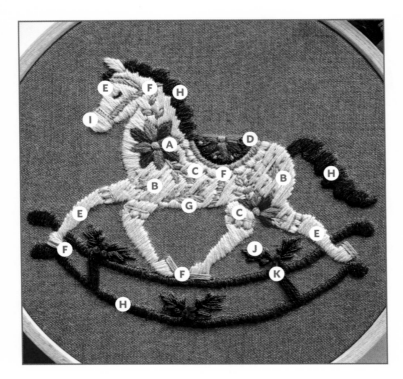

STITCH GUIDE

A 3831 and 815, satin leaf stitch, 3 strands (petals); 3347, satin stitch, 3 strands (centers)

B 3828, satin stitch, 3 strands

C 739, satin stitch, 3 strands (inside scallops); and 3828, back stitch, 3 strands (for outline)

D 320 and 3828, satin stitch and cross knots, 3 strands

E 3033, satin stitch and satin leaf stitch, 3 strands

F 3828, satin stitch and back stitch, 3 strands

G 320, whipped back stitch and satin leaf stitch, 3 strands

H 938, satin stitch, 3 strands

I 938, back stitch, 3 strands

J 319, holly leaf stitch, 3 strands

K 815, French knots, 6 strands

INSTRUCTIONS

TIP **for Satin Stitching the Horse:** As there is a great deal of satin stitch for the horse's body, I would recommend stitching the other elements first (flowers, saddle, bands, stars without the surrounding lines) and then referencing the grey directional lines on the pattern template when working on the satin stitch body.

1. Start the pattern by stitching the poinsettia flowers with three strands of the two reds (3831, 815) and a satin leaf stitch. Continue by filling in their centers with three-stranded satin stitches in the bright green shade (3347) (**A**).

2. Next, stitch the gold (3828) diamond stars on the horse's front and back leg (**B**). Start with a three-stranded satin stitch down the middle and work your way out on either side, making sure to shorten your stitches to finish the edges of the star.

3. Stitch the scalloped bands on the horse's legs and around the saddle with the light yellow (739) and a three-stranded satin stitch (**C**). Start with a stitch down the middle and work your way out to fill out the curved shapes.

4. Next, stitch the green (320) base of the saddle with a three-stranded satin stitch, working your way along the grey directional lines and finishing with three-stranded cross knots on top using the gold floss (3828). Connect the scalloped edges to the green saddle by using a three-stranded satin stitch to fill in the band with the same gold shade (3828) (**D**).

5. Now that you've filled in all the motifs on the horse, it's time to fill in the white (3033) satin stitch base (**E**). Start from the muzzle and work your way up the head, making sure to stitch around the bands. Use a three-stranded satin leaf stitch to fill in the horse's ear. Continue with a satin stitch down the neck and across the body, and down the legs and toward the tail. Be careful to keep the satin stitch close around the elements you've already stitched and be mindful about leaving the remaining leafy vine outlines open to fill in later.

6. Use three strands of the gold shade (3828) to fill in the remaining gold bands on the horse's head and stomach with a satin stitch. You can also go ahead and use a three-strand back stitch to fill out the directional "shining" lines around the stars (**F**).

   TIP for Stitching the Gold Bands: Run your satin stitch at a slight diagonal to give a "braided" look to the bands. Start with the horizontal bands and then move on to the vertical when you're stitching the head bands of the horse. For the middle band across the stomach, start at the bottom and work your way up between the scalloped bands.

7. Use the warm-green shade (320) to fill in the remaining leafy vines with a combination of three-stranded whipped back stitches and satin leaf stitches (**G**).

TIP for Stitching the Leafy Vines: These leafy details in particular are a bit easier to stitch over the white satin stitch of the horse after you've filled in the horse's white body. You can stitch them in whatever order that you'd like, but I find this method to work best, especially with the whipped back stitch vines layered on top of the satin stitch.

8. Fill in the hair of the horse's mane and tail. Use three strands of the brown shade (938) and a satin stitch to fill in the mane starting from the top of the horse's head (**H**). Run a stitch down the middle and work your way out on either side to fill out the scalloped edges. Work your way down the mane, following the grey directional lines to keep it even until the bottom curve. Start at the top of the horse's tail and run down to the bottom curve, as well.

9. Use the same brown shade (938) and a three-stranded back stitch to fill in the line details of the eye and nose (**I**). You might need to use multiple tiny stitches to get the curved effect you desire, but you can also use your needle to push up on the stitch slightly until you're happy with the curved shape.

10. From here you'll continue stitching with the same brown shade (938) and the same satin stitching method to fill out the wooden base of the horse (**H**). Start at whichever curved end you'd like and work your way across the arches, running your stitches vertically and all the way down to where the two arches connect, making sure to stitch the vertical connecting slats as you go.

11. Finish off your horse by stitching the golden hooves using a satin stitch and three strands of the gold shade (3828) (**B**). Stitch the holly berries on the base using three-stranded holly leaf stitches with the dark-green (319) (**J**) and six-stranded French knots with the red shade (815) (**K**).

Rainbow Snow Globe

THERE'S SOMETHING SO FESTIVE AND WINTERY about a cute snow globe in general, but add in some mini trees, a few rainbow fairy lights, and the satiny shine of embroidery floss and you've got yourself a pretty magical Christmas pattern! Because the rainbow lights take up most of the free space in this little globe, the fluffy snow is simply resting on the base. But all of the details and textures still do a good job of capturing that specialness of this iconic holiday motif. This design is probably one of the most complex patterns in the book next to the Christmas Cabin and features a good bit of satin stitching, back stitching, and French knots; but the end result is well worth the time it will take! Due to the number of French knots on this piece, I would recommend it as a stationary piece of artwork; but if you use the faux French-knot method when stitching the snow and lights, it'll make it a lot more stable for use on a piece of clothing or a washable item like a tea towel.

MATERIALS

- 7" Square of Fabric (I used Kona cotton in the shade White)
- Embroidery Floss (see colour guide for suggested hues)
- Embroidery Hoop (5" or 13 cm)
- Embroidery Snips/Scissors
- Pattern Transferring Tools + Transfer Method of Choice
- Size 5 Embroidery Needle

COLOUR GUIDE

- Blanc
- 3866
- 3033
- 738
- 3045
- 369
- 368
- 989

- 3862
- 152
- 3772
- 309
- 3687
- 3854
- 562
- 826

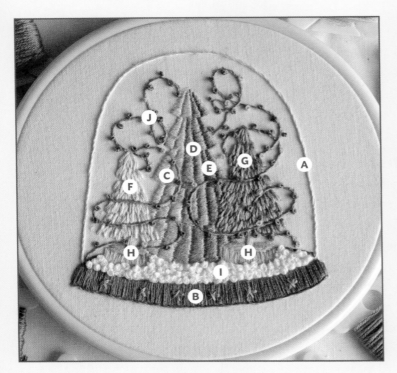

STITCH GUIDE

A 3866, whipped back stitch, 3 strands

B 3862, satin stitch, 3 strands; 3045, whipped back stitch (base) and back stitch (stars), 3 strands

C 369, satin stitch, 3 strands

D 368, satin stitch, 3 strands

E 989, satin stitch, 3 strands

F 3866 and 3033, back stitch, 6 strands

G 152 and 3772, back stitch, 6 strands

H 738, satin stitch, 3 strands

I Blanc, French knots, 6 strands

J 3045, whipped back stitch, 3 strands (light string); 309, 3687, 562, 826 and 3854, French knots, 6 strands

INSTRUCTIONS

1. Start the pattern by stitching the outline of the snow globe with the cool white (3866) and a three-stranded whipped back stitch (**A**).

2. Next, satin stitch the base of the globe with three strands of the brown shade (3862). I recommend starting in the center of the globe and stitching from side to side with your satin stitch method of choice. You'll then go back in with three strands of the gold shade (3045) and a back stitch to stitch the stars. Finish off the base by outlining the bottom edge with three strands of the same gold shade and a whipped back stitch (**B**).

TIP for Stitching the Gold Stars on the Base: Before you stitch over your star outlines, make a tiny mark under the base to note the locations of your stars. Once you've satin stitched the brown base, you'll go back in to add the tiny gold stars. Start with a horizontal stitch (about a cm wide) and pull down gently so you don't create gaps in your satin stitches. Then go back in and cross your horizontal lines with diagonal stitches to complete your stars.

3. Satin stitch the center green tree. Start with three strands of the lightest green shade (369) to get the top of the tree started. Work your

way down with horizontal satin stitches, filling in each vertical rib of the tree as you go (**C**). You can reference the original pattern photo as you're going, but you'll want to fill in the first two vertical ribs (side by side) from top to bottom on the far left with the lightest green shade (369) first. When you get to the bottom and the ribs start to mesh with the other trees, just satin stitch around their edges.

TIP for Stitching Around the String of Lights: When you're satin stitching or back stitching down the tree ribs, simply run your stitches up to the string template lines instead of over them. This should leave you with a faint string outline that you can back stitch overtop of. See how to layer your stitches on page 61 for photo examples.

4. Next, use three strands of the middle green shade (368) to fill in the third vertical rib at the top of the tree and the middle two ribs, working all the way down (**D**).

5. Finish the tree with three strands of the final green shade (989). Satin stitch the last rib of the top of the tree and work your way down until you reach the bottom (**E**). When you get to the bottom and the ribs start to mesh with the other trees, just satin stitch around their edges.

6. Move on to the bottle brush trees. Start with the white one on the left and use six strands of the cool white (3866) and a back stitch to fill in the outline all the way down, making sure to leave the string outline uncovered. Go back in with six strands of the warmer cream colour (3033) to fill in any gaps in the tree and give it a fuller look (**F**).

7. Next, stitch the mauve tree on the right. Start by using six strands of the light mauve (152) and a back stitch to fill in the tree outline all the way down, making sure to leave the string outline uncovered. Go back in with six strands of the darker mauve (3772) to fill in any gaps in the tree and give it the same fuller look (**G**).

8. Next, stitch the light wooden bases of your bottle brush trees. Use three strands of the light tan shade (738) to satin stitch the base following the grey directional lines on the template. Start with the bottom of the base, followed by the top, and then the vertical post (**H**).

9. Now that your trees are all stitched, your next step is to fill in the floor of the wooden base with the French knot snow! Use six strands of the white shade (Blanc) to fill in the base, starting with an outline around the whole snow area and filling in the middle. Add as many French knots as you'd like in order to give the base the fluffiest look possible (**I**). You can also add back stitches around the edges and trees to fill any gaps left over. Alternatively, you can simply satin stitch in the snow or leave the base open if you used a lighter fabric!

10. The next step is to stitch the fairy lights! You'll use three strands of the gold shade (3045) and a back stitch to trace the outline from the left base of the globe, up and around all the trees, and back down to the right (**J**). Then go back in and use the same strand to whip the back stitch, making sure to bring your needle under from the right side each time. This will create a clean line for you to add your French knot lights onto.

11. Lastly, add in your coloured fairy lights! Using six strands of the five rainbow colours (309, 3687, 3854, 562, 826) you'll fill in the dotted lights with French knots (**J**). You'll need to do these individually with each colour to keep your French knots from pulling, so I would recommend starting at the bottom and working your way around the string with one colour at a time. I followed a colour pattern of red, pink, orange, green, blue. Alternatively, if you would prefer white lights, you can use the light-yellow shade (738) to stitch your French knots instead.

Pretty Poinsettia

WHEN I FIRST STARTED CREATING ORIGINAL PATTERNS, I created one called Magical Magenta that featured a half moon arch; a gorgeous colour palette of pinks, greens, and magentas; and a bunch of woven roses. It became one of my best-selling patterns and inspired several different seasonal takes, including Bells and Blooms, Web of Roses, and this pattern, Pretty Poinsettia. It's a gorgeous pattern of holly berries, mistletoe, pine needles, and, of course, some vibrant red roses. It would make a beautiful addition to a tea towel or apron and features a nice gap for adding in a family name or classic Christmas saying. If you're going to stitch it on a high-use garment, I would recommend using the faux French knots for the berries so they'll be more secure when washing.

MATERIALS

- 8" Square of Fabric (I used Kona cotton in the shade White)
- Embroidery Floss (see colour guide for suggested shades)
- Embroidery Hoop (6" or 15 cm)
- Embroidery Snips/Scissors
- Pattern Transferring Tools + Transfer Method of Choice
- Size 5 Embroidery Needle

COLOUR GUIDE

- Blanc
- 3831
- 3350
- 3685
- 524
- 523
- 3053
- 3011
- 936
- 3787

A 3053 and 3787, satin leaf stitch, 3 strands

B 3011, holly leaf stitch, 3 strands

C 936, back stitch, 6 strands

D 523, lazy daisy branch, 6 strands

E 524, whipped back stitch and satin leaf stitch, 3 strands; Blanc, French knots, 6 strands

F Blanc, 3350, and 3685, satin leaf stitch, 3 strands

G 524, cross knots and satin stitch, 3 strands

H Blanc and 3685, satin stitch, 3 strands

I 3685, woven wheel rose, 6 strands

J 3350, woven wheel rose, 6 strands

K 3831, woven wheel rose, 6 strands

L Blanc and 3685, French knots, 6 strands

INSTRUCTIONS

1. Start by stitching the greenery. Use three strands of both light and pale green shades (3053, 3787) and a satin leaf stitch to create all the leaves around the roses and poinsettia flowers (**A**).

2. Use the darker green shade (3011) and a three-stranded holly leaf stitch for the leaves of all the holly berries (**B**). Start with a straight stitch from the top to one third of the way down the center of the leaf and then proceed with the crisscrossing stitches following the curves of the leaf.

3. Stitch the straight-lined pine needles with a three-stranded back stitch using the darkest green shade (936) (**C**). You can also use six strands if you'd prefer thicker pine needles.

4. Next up are the loopy lazy daisy branches with the cool green shade (523). Make sure to stitch the stems of the branches with a whipped back stitch first and then go in with your lazy daisy leaves up the branch (**D**).

5. Your last bit of greenery will be tackling the warmer green branches with the mistletoe berries. Start by whipped back stitching the stems of the branches with three strands of the warmer green shade (524) then go back in with a satin leaf stitch for the leaves (**E**). Finish off these branches by going in with three strands of the white (Blanc) for the French knot mistletoe berries. You can also leave the French knot berries until the very end!

6. Next up is the poinsettia flowers. Start by stitching the white flowers with three strands of the white shade (Blanc) and a satin leaf stitch. Then go in with both red shades (3350, 3685) to stitch the petals of the red flowers with the same satin leaf method (**F**). You'll then use three strands of the light green shade (524) to fill in all of the red flower centers with cross knot stitches. Finish off the centers of the white flowers using the same 3 strands of green (524) and a satin stitch (**G**).

7. Now you'll focus on stitching the candy canes. You'll want to start with three strands of the white (Blanc) and a horizontal satin stitch at the shorter curved end of the stick. Continue by satin stitching all other white parts, following the curve of the cane. Finish off your canes by satin stitching the rest of the red parts with three strands of the dark red (3685) (**H**).

8. Lastly, fill in the woven roses with the three vibrant shades of red (3685, 3350, 3831) and six-stranded woven wheel rose stitches (**I–K**). Make sure to keep your center weaving loose and use overlapping stitches to give your roses a fluffier, fuller look! You can also use your needle to gently shape the petals.

9. At this point you'll want to go in with the white (Blanc) and dark red (3685) to fill in any remaining mistletoe and holly berries with 6-stranded French knots (**L**). Make sure to use the faux French knot method if you're stitching on high-use garments!

Citrus and Berries

THERE'S SOMETHING SO FRESH AND FESTIVE about an orange and berry wreath for the holidays! I loved the idea of incorporating more coral and brighter pink tones to stitch up raspberry oranges in addition to the classic mandarin ones. This wreath incorporates lazy daisy stems and leafy branches full of dark-red berries to finish the wreath. The pattern also uses satin-stitched centers and chain-stitched borders to add extra texture to the finished artwork. This design would be gorgeous on a tea towel or on a linen bag to store or gift some fresh oranges in! Just make sure, if you're stitching this design on a garment that will get a lot of use, to use the faux-French-knot method for the berries so that they are more durable for washing. If you're more of a traditional orange lover, simply replace the red and coral colours for the orange ones.

MATERIALS

- 8" Square of Fabric (I used Kona cotton in the shade Natural)
- Embroidery Floss (see colour guide for suggested hues)
- Embroidery Hoop (6" or 15 cm)
- Embroidery Snips/Scissors
- Pattern Transferring Tools + Transfer Method of Choice
- Size 5 Embroidery Needle

COLOUR GUIDE

- 352
- 3705
- 815
- 976
- 977
- 19
- 369
- 3053
- 523
- 3346

STITCH GUIDE

A 3053 and 523, lazy daisy branch, 6 strands

B 369, whipped back stitch and satin leaf stitch, 3 strands; 352, satin stitch, 3 strands

C 3346, whipped back stitch and satin leaf stitch, 3 strands; 815, French knots, 6 strands

D 19 and 815, satin stitch, 3 strands

E 977 and 3705, back stitch, 6 strands (lines)

F 977 and 3705, chain stitch, 6 strands

G 976 and 352, chain stitch, 6 strands

H 976, back stitch, 3 strands

INSTRUCTIONS

1. Start the pattern by using three strands of the two light-green shades (3053, 523) and a lazy daisy branch stitch for the loopy branches around the wreath (**A**).

2. Next, use the lightest green shade (369) to stitch the stems and leaves of the coral flowers with a three-stranded whipped back stitch and satin leaf stitch. Afterward, you can go in with three strands of the coral shade (352) with a satin stitch to finish off the flowers on the same stems (**B**).

3. Finish the greenery by stitching the remaining berry branches with three strands of the darkest green (3346) and a combination of the whipped back stitch and satin leaf stitch (**C**). You can save the French knot berries until the end so you don't pull them as you continue stitching.

4. Next up is stitching the oranges! Stitch the orange triangles one at a time by stitching a line down the center of each orange and working your way out on either side to fill them in with a three-stranded satin stitch following the grey directional lines. You'll want to use the lightest orange (19) and the darkest red (815) to fill in these triangles around the wreath (**D**).

5. Use a six-stranded back stitch with the medium orange (977) and hot pink (3705) to stitch the separated detail lines over the top of the satin-stitched centers (**E**). Start your stitches from the outside edges of each triangle and pull them down in the center so as to not catch the middle stitches while you stitch all six lines.

TIP **for Stitching the Orange Slices:** After you've satin stitched the orange centers, make sure to do the back-stitched detail lines over the top of the wedges to separate them. Then follow up with the chain-stitched orange borders to cover the stitches.

6. Stitch the inner borders of your oranges using the medium orange (977) and hot pink (3705) with a six-stranded chain stitch to fill in the inner border (**F**).

TIP **for a Seamless Chain-Stitched Border for the Oranges:** When you chain stitch the border of your orange and get all the way around to your initial stitch, pull your needle up and instead of making a loop to pull the stitch through, simply run your needle under the initial loop of your first chain and then pull your needle down its last hole to finish the seamless loop.

7. Finally, finish your oranges by using the darkest orange (976) and coral pink (352) with a six-stranded chain stitch to fill in the outer border (**G**). Finish the star-shaped flourishes with 3-stranded back stitches of the same colour (976) (**H**).

8. If you've left your French knot berries until the end, now is the time to finish filling them in with the darkest red (815) and a six-stranded French knot (**C**). If you've decided to stitch the wreath on a garment that will get a lot of use, make sure to use the faux-French-knot method for the berries so that they are more durable for washing.

Candy Cane Blooms

WHEN I FIRST STARTED DISCOVERING MY SIGNATURE STYLE of crafting objects out of florals, it became a really fun game of how to get creative with the floral placements and colours. The Candy Cane Blooms pattern was a result of my first shot at mixing this signature style with some holiday magic. It's a bit of a complex pattern in that it uses various shades of red and white to craft the iconic motif, but the overall finished pattern is full of depth and colour that creates a great candy cane illusion. This pattern would work beautifully on the corner of a tea towel, on the giant pocket of an apron, or simply as a lovely Christmas artwork. I stitched this pattern in an oval hoop as it worked better for its scale, but you can also use an 8" hoop for a fuller canvas or for while you're stitching. Just be mindful of maintaining good fabric tension (which is especially important for bigger hoops with a greater fabric surface).

MATERIALS

- 10" × 7" Rectangle or 10" × 10" Square of Fabric (I used Kona cotton in the shade White)
- Embroidery Floss (see colour guide for suggested hues)
- Embroidery Hoop (8" × 5" oval or 8" × 8" circular hoop)
- Embroidery Snips/Scissors
- Pattern Transferring Tools + Transfer Method of Choice
- Size 5 Embroidery Needle

COLOUR GUIDE

- Blanc
- 3866
- 3832
- 3831
- 777
- 814

STITCH GUIDE

A Blanc, satin leaf stitch, 3 strands

B Blanc, whipped back stitch and satin leaf stitch, 3 strands (leaves); 3866, satin stitch, 3 strands (petals)

C 3866, satin leaf stitch, 3 strands

D 3866, whipped back stitch and satin leaf stitch, 3 strands (leaves); 3866 and Blanc, satin leaf stitch, 3 strands (petals)

E Blanc, whipped backstitch and satin leaf stitch, 3 strands

F Blanc and 3866, satin leaf stitch, 3 strands

G Blanc, satin leaf stitch, 3 strands

H 777 and 3831, satin leaf stitch, 3 strands

I 3832, whipped backstitch and satin leaf stitch, 3 strands

J 777 and 814, satin leaf stitch, 3 strands

K 814, whipped backstitch and satin leaf stitch, 3 strands (leaves); 3832, satin stitch, 3 strands (petals)

L 814, whipped backstitch and satin leaf stitch, 3 strands (leaves); 777 and 3832, satin leaf stitch, 3 strands (petals)

M 777 and 3831, satin leaf stitch, 3 strands

N 3832, satin leaf stitch, 3 strands

O 3866, satin leaf stitch, 3 strands (rose); Blanc, woven wheel rose, 6 strands (rose)

P 3866 and Blanc, satin leaf stitch, 3 strands; Blanc, woven wheel rose, 6 strands (rose)

Q 3831 and 777, satin leaf stitch, 3 strands; 814, woven wheel rose, 6 strands

R 3831 and 777, satin leaf stitch, 3 strands; 814, woven wheel rose, 6 strands (rose)

S 777 and 814, satin leaf stitch (leaves); 3831, woven wheel rose, 6 strands (rose)

T Blanc and 814, whipped back stitch, 3 strands

INSTRUCTIONS

1. Start off by stitching all the white parts of the candy cane first. Each one varies slightly, so you'll need to look at each section and its numbered parts to identify which element needs which colour—either white (Blanc) or off white (3866) (**A–G**). Fill in each stem, leaf, and flower petal with a mix of three-strand whipped back stitches and satin leaf stitches. Make sure to leave the roses for last, so they don't catch as you continue stitching.

   TIP for Stitching Smaller Flowers: With the tiniest flowers being so delicate, you may just need a back stitch or two to fill in the petals and leaves as opposed to a full satin leaf stitch.

2. Next, fill in the red sections of the candy cane with the same method as above, but make sure to note which sections use what combination of the four reds (3832, 3831, 777, 814) (**H–N**). Use the same combination of three-stranded whipped back stitches and satin leaf stitches to fill in the stems, leaves, and flower petals. Make sure to leave the roses for last.

3. Finish stitching the last couple of woven roses in the white section with six strands of the white (Blanc) and the three-spoke method of woven rose stitching (**O–P**). Make sure to keep your center weaving loose and use overlapping stitches to give your roses a fluffier and fuller look. You can also use your needle to gently shape the petals.

4. Next, finish the rest of the woven roses in the red section with six strands of various reds (3832, 3831, 814) and the three-spoke method of woven rose stitching (**Q–S**). Make sure to keep your center weaving loose and use over-lapping stitches to give your roses a fluffier and fuller look. You can also use your needle to gently shape the petals.

5. The last thing you'll do to finish your candy cane is go in and stitch the borders with a three-stranded whipped back stitch and a mixture of the white (Blanc) and dark red (814), making sure to stitch up to and flush with the other elements of the red and white sections you've already stitched (**T**).

   TIP for Stitching the Candy Cane Outline: Stitch the outlining border of each section last after filling in all of the sections, being careful to run each line flat up against the other elements' edges (as opposed to around it or over the top) for a smooth finish.

Feathers and Florals

AN ANGEL ON TOP OF THE CHRISTMAS TREE is such a classic Christmas motif, I had to add it to my pattern list when I was brainstorming festive patterns for this book. Growing up, my grandma had a beautiful handmade angel on her tree with white lace and soft details. I took inspiration from that memory and some creative liberties to craft an angel with a unique dress made of florals. My signature style combined with the soft creams, warm greens, and vibrant reds makes for a stunning angel, perfect for adorning your favourite tea towel, linen bag, or holiday gallery wall. Angels come in all different forms, so I've included some additional skin and hair tones for you to customize your own angel as you see fit—but it might also be easier to visit your local craft store to see the wide array of tones available!

MATERIALS

- 9" Square of Fabric (I used Kona cotton in the shade White)
- Embroidery Floss (see colour guide for suggested hues)
- Embroidery Hoop (7" or 18 cm)
- Embroidery Snips/Scissors
- Pattern Transferring Tools + Transfer Method of Choice
- Size 5 Embroidery Needle

COLOUR GUIDE

Pattern Palette

- 3865
- 3866
- 951
- 437
- 801
- 326
- 3685
- 778
- 524
- 522
- 3362

Skin and Hair Palette

- 951
- 3864
- 3862
- 435
- 400
- 801
- 839
- 938
- 310

STITCH GUIDE

A A colour for the skin (I used 951), satin stitch, 3 strands

B A colour for the hair (I used 801), satin stitch, 3 strands

C 437, whipped back stitch, 3 strands

D 3865, whipped back stitch, 3 strands

E 3866, whipped back stitch and satin leaf stitch, 3 strands; 3865, wavy petal stitch, 3 strands

F 524 and 522, satin leaf stitch, 3 strands

G 3362, whipped back stitch and satin leaf stitch, 3 strands (stems)

H 778, wavy petal stitch, 3 strands

I 3685, satin stitch and satin leaf stitch, 3 strands

J 3865, satin leaf stitch, 3 strands

K 326, woven wheel rose, 6 strands

INSTRUCTIONS

1. Start by stitching in the face and hands of the angel with three strands of your chosen skin tone (**A**). Start at the top center of the angel's head and run a stitch down the middle, working your way out on either side with the satin stitch method of your choice and following the directional lines. Use the same satin stitching method for stitching in the hands, as well.

2. Fill in the hair with three strands of your chosen hair colour, starting with a stitch down the middle and working your way out on either side, following the directional lines and the curves of the hair (**B**). Don't forget to stitch the lower edges of the hair peeking out from under the angel's dress sleeves, too.

3. Stitch the angel's halo with the gold shade (437) and a three-stranded whipped back stitch (**C**).

4. Next, you'll start stitching the angel's wings with a three-stranded whipped back stitch and the warm white shade (3865), starting at the top arches of the wings nearest the hair (**D**). Start with a normal back stitch and work your way down, layer by layer, to the bottom tips. Work on one layer of wings at a time and run your back stitch down and around each curved feather. This will make whipping the back-stitched feathers a lot easier.

5. The next step is to start working on the angel's dress, beginning with the white and off-white elements. Use three strands of the off white (3866) to fill in the leafy vines around the dress with whipped back stitches and satin leaf stitches. Continue by also filling in the white flowers with three strands of the warm white shade (3865) and a wavy petal stitch (**E**). Finish off the white flowers by satin stitching the centers with three strands of the gold shade (437) (**C**).

TIP **for Stitching the Angel Dress Outline:**
Stitch the outlining border of the dress last after filling in the other elements, including the leaves, flowers, and roses, as their forms will help to define some of the dress's edges and overall shape. Be mindful about running each line flat up against the other element edges (as opposed to around it or over the top of it) for a smooth finish.

6. Continue by filling in the greenery of the dress. Use the two shades of the lighter greens (524, 522) and fill in the full individual leaves around the dress with a three-stranded satin leaf stitch (**F**). Then go in with the darkest green (3362) and fill in the remaining leafy vines with the same three-stranded whipped back stitch and satin leaf stitch (**G**).

7. From here you can fill in the remaining purple wavy flowers with a combination of the mauve purple shade (778) and a three-stranded wavy petal stitch (**H**). Fill in the centers with a three-stranded satin stitch in the darker burgundy shade (3685) (**I**). Finish off any remaining flower petals with the same burgundy (3685) and a satin leaf stitch, with the exception of the middle flowers (which you'll fill with three strands of the warm white (3865)) (**J**).

8. Fill in the woven roses with six strands of the vibrant red (326) and a mixture of the three-spoke and five-spoke woven rose stitches (**K**). Make sure to keep your center weave loose and use overlapping stitches to give your roses a fluffier and fuller look. You can also use your needle to gently shape the petals.

TIP **for Stitching the Roses:** If you find that the three-pronged roses are giving you trouble, you can try stitching them as five-pronged ones instead for a more stable base. Just use three strands for your initial prongs, and make sure your rose doesn't get too bulky!

9. Lastly, tie your whole angel dress together by stitching the outline with a whipped back stitch and three strands of the warm white shade (3865) (**D**).

Bows and Baubles

WHAT IS A BOOK OF CHRISTMAS EMBROIDERY PATTERNS without an iconic Christmas tree? I created this pattern after seeing a bunch of adorable trees decked out with velvet and satin ribbons over the last few years. The design also features coloured baubles, which is a charming European term for ornaments or a word that means "small, showy decorations." I used a variety of pretty soft pinks and purples paired with rich greens and blues to contrast beautifully with the vibrant pink ribbons. Feel free to alter the colours of the bows and baubles as you see fit, but I highly recommend using a lighter-coloured fabric to keep with the fun and playful vibe of this pattern. It would be a lovely addition to any sweater, stocking, or tea towel, and features simple stitches that are all super durable for washing and wearing. This might be one of my favourite patterns in the book, but who doesn't love a classic Christmas tree?

MATERIALS

- 9" Square of Fabric (I used Kona cotton in the shade Bellini)
- Embroidery Floss (see colour guide for suggested hues)
- Embroidery Hoop (7" or 18 cm)
- Embroidery Snips/Scissors
- Pattern Transferring Tools + Transfer Method of Choice
- Size 5 Embroidery Needle

COLOUR GUIDE

- 225
- 3727
- 3836
- 31
- 3726
- 3350
- E436
- 801
- 3345
- 989
- 523

STITCH GUIDE

A 523, 989, and 3345, back stitch, 6 strands

B E436, satin stitch, 1 strand

C 3727, 3836, 3345, and 31, satin stitch, 3 strands

D 801, satin stitch, 3 strands

E 3836 and 3726, satin stitch, 3 strands

F 225 and 3350, lazy daisy loops and whipped back stitch, 6 strands

INSTRUCTIONS

NOTE **About the Metallic Floss (E436) for the Star:** If you're not a fan of metallic floss, simply use the normal floss shade 436 in its place—just remember to stitch with three strands of the gold colour in the place of one strand of the metallic floss!

1. Start off this pattern by stitching the base layer of the tree with six-stranded back stitches using the darkest green shade (3345). Start from the top tip of the tree and work your way down to the bottom edges filling in the black lines of the branches (**A**).

2. Next, go in with six strands of the medium green shade (989) and add in additional back stitches all around the darker green lines you've just stitched (**A**). Make sure to keep your stitches running in the same direction as the initial darker lines, but don't totally fill in all the spare space, as you'll go in with a lighter shade for highlights. Start from the top tip of the tree and work your way down to the bottom edges, as above.

3. Take six strands of the lightest green shade (523) and use a back stitch to fill in the remainder of any gaps left in your tree. This will give it a completely filled look and lend extra dimension to your tree. Start from the top tip of the tree and work your way down to the bottom edges (**A**).

4. Use one strand of the metallic gold floss (E436) to satin stitch the star (**B**). The reason I recommend using one strand of this shade is because metallic floss is notoriously hard to stitch with as it tangles and frays easily. I find using one strand helps to counteract this and makes working with the floss a lot easier.

5. Next, stitch the baubles with a three-stranded satin stitch and the multiple colours (3727, 3836, 3345, 31) (**C**). You'll want to stitch these the same way as a normal satin stitch circle with a stitch down the middle and by working your way out on either side.

6. From here you can fill in the trunk of the tree with the brown shade (801) and a three-stranded satin stitch (**D**). You'll want to start at the base of the tree and run your long stitches up and down to fill out the shape. I would recommend using the second method of satin stitching so your stitches lie fairly flat—just make sure not to pull them too tight.

7. Use the cool purple (3836) and mauve pink (3726) to fill out the tree skirt with a three-stranded satin stitch (**E**). You'll want to stitch the purple base first and then stitch the mauve border after, running your needle up at the bottom edge and down against the purple base. I recommend starting in the middle of the skirt and working your way out, following the grey directional lines.

8. Lastly, you'll finish your tree by stitching in the bows. You'll use six strands of the lightest pink (225) and the vibrant pink (3350) to fill in the outlines you previously left (**I, J**). Start by using lazy daisy loops to fill in the bow loops and finish by using a whipped back stitch for the bow tails. Make sure to use smaller back stitches so you're able to loop the bow's shorter tails.

Stuffed Stocking

THIS STUFFED STOCKING PATTERN is still one of my proudest holiday-pattern achievements to date. I created it as I was dreaming of what other festive objects I could shape with florals! As I was sketching out the tiny blooms across the stocking's form, I was trying to think of ways I could separate the top band and bottom tip from the full stockings shape without stitching a definitive line. If you look closely and also from a distance, you can see that I was able to achieve this goal by using lighter pastel shades for the top band and bottom curved tip. The center of the stocking features darker and richer colours, and all together you get one magical stuffed stocking full of all the Christmas elements. Featuring a beautiful colour palette of reds, greens, and gold; and various festive foliage from holly berries to pine needles, this pattern is sure to be a marvel any way you use it. It would look amazing on a tea towel, drawstring linen pouch, or even stitched on the center of a larger linen stocking. Just make sure that if you're stitching it on a garment that will get more use, use the faux French knots so they will be more durable for washing. Even though this pattern is truly "stuffed" full of all the festive elements and may take you a little while to stitch, it's a great project to work away at over the holiday season!

MATERIALS

- 9" Square of Fabric (I used Kona cotton in the shade Natural)
- Embroidery Floss (see colour guide for suggested hues)
- Embroidery Hoop (7" or 18 cm)
- Embroidery Snips/Scissors
- Pattern Transferring Tools + Transfer Method of Choice
- Size 5 Embroidery Needle

COLOUR GUIDE

3866	777
739	902
3856	3053
435	471
223	580
3721	3362
3831	319

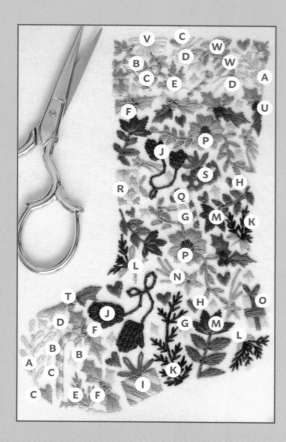

STITCH GUIDE

A 3866, lazy daisy branch, 3 strands

B 3866, satin stitch, 3 strands

C 223, satin stitch, 3 strands

D 739, satin leaf stitch and whipped back stitch, 3 strands

E 3866 and 471, back stitch and lazy daisy stitch, 3 strands

F 3053 and 580, holly leaf stitch, 3 strands; 223, French knots, 6 strands

G 3856, satin stitch, 3 strands

H 3721, satin stitch, 3 strands

I 3866 and 223, satin stitch, 3 strands; 3831, lazy daisy stitch, 6 strands

J 902, chain stitch and whipped back stitch, 3 strands

K 319, back stitch, 3 strands

L 435, satin leaf stitch and whipped back stitch, 3 strands

M 3362, whipped back stitch and satin leaf stitch, 3 strands; 777, satin leaf stitch, 3 strands; 3831, back stitch, 3 strands (for lines)

N 435, satin leaf stitch and whipped back stitch, 3 strands

O 3866 and 580, satin stitch, 3 strands; 580, lazy daisy stitch, 6 strands

P 223, wavy petal stitch, 3 strands; 3721, satin stitch, 3 strands; 3053, lazy daisy branch stitch, 3 strands

Q 3866 and 3721, satin stitch, 3 strands

R 739, satin stitch, 3 strands; 435, back stitch and lazy daisy stitch, 3 strands

S 580 and 3866, satin stitch, 3 strands; 3831, lazy daisy stitch, 6 strands

T 3053 and 580, holly leaf stitch, 3 strands; 223, French knots, 6 strands

U 3053 and 580, holly leaf stitch, 3 strands; 777, French knots, 6 strands

V 3866, wavy petal stitch, 3 strands

W 471 and 3053, satin stitch, 3 strands

INSTRUCTIONS

1. Start by stitching in the lighter elements at the left base of the stocking's tip. Use the cool white shade (3866) to fill in the loopy branches with three strands and a lazy daisy branch (**A**). Fill in the white sections of the nearest candy cane with the same white (3866) and a three-stranded satin stitch. Then stitch the tiny diamond stars with a three-stranded satin stitch by running a stitch down the middle and filling out either side with the same white shade (**B**).

2. Use the light pink (223) to fill in the heart with a three-stranded satin stitch. Continue with the same colour and fill in the remaining pink sections of the nearest candy cane with the same pink shade (223) and a three-stranded satin stitch (**C**).

3. Use the lightest yellow shade (739) with a three-stranded satin leaf stitch and whipped back stitch to fill in the star (**D**).

   TIP for Stitching the Satin Leaf Stitch Stars: Start by running a stitch from the point of each star's tip to the center of the shape. Fill in the space on either side of each line by using the satin leaf stitch method and following the sharper edges of the stars.

4. Fill in the little pine needle details using three strands of the warm green (471) and a back stitch. Finish off the detail by using three strands of the white shade (3866) and a mix of a lazy daisy loop and a back stitch to fill in the box over the top (**E**).

5. Fill in the last details of the lighter tip by stitching in the holly berry details. Start by using the lightest green (3053) and a three-stranded holly leaf stitch to fill in the majority of the leaves. You'll notice there's one additional leaf on the top right that is a darker green shade. Stitch this remaining leaf with the darker green shade (580) and the same three-strand holly leaf technique. Finish off the holly berries by using the pink shade (223) and six-stranded French knots (**F**).

6. Next, fill in the more vibrant base of the stocking. Start off with the soft yellow (3856) and a three-stranded satin stitch to fill out the diamond stars all around the middle of the stocking (**G**). Run a stitch down the middle and fill out either side, shortening your stitches as you go.

7. Go in with the pastel red (3721) and a satin stitch to fill in the hearts all around the middle of the stocking. Start with a stitch down the middle and work your way out on either side to fill in the shapes (**H**).

8. From here, fill in the striped present on the bottom left. Use three strands of the cool white (3866) and the light pink (223) with a three-stranded satin stitch to fill out the stripes of the stocking. Then use the bright red (3831) to finish the present with six-stranded lazy daisy loops for the bow (**I**).

9. Use the darkest burgundy shade (902) with a three-stranded chain stitch to fill in the mitten bases (**J**). Finish off the pair with a three-stranded whipped back stitch to finish the loopy string that attaches them together. Fill in the second set of mittens above with the same stitching technique.

continued . . .

. . . continued

TIP for Stitching the Mittens: Start at the flat base of the mitten and work your way up the center grey line, filling in the line with a chain stitch until you reach the top. Fill in the rest of the mitten with a chain stitch on either side (still starting at the flat base) and finish with the thumb piece.

10. Next up, focus on stitching in the darker pine branches, and the ones tied with bows. Use three strands of the darkest green (319) and a back stitch to fill in the pine branches all around the middle of the stocking (**K**). Then, go back in with three strands of the gold shade (435) with a combination of satin leaf and whipped back stitches to finish off the bows on the tied branches (**L**).

11. Fill in the red pointed flowers around the middle of the stocking. Start by using three strands of the cool green (3362) with a combination of a whipped back stitch and satin leaf stitch to fill in the stems of the flowers. Then use three strands of the darker red (777) with a three-stranded satin leaf stitch to fill in the petals. Finish off the petals with the brighter red shade (3831) and a three-stranded back stitch over the top, running you stitches from the center of the petals to the base (**M**).

12. Use the gold shade (435) with a three-stranded satin leaf stitch and whipped back stitch to fill in the stars in the middle of the stocking (**N**).

13. Fill in the white and green wrapped present with a three-stranded satin stitch to fill in the base. Use the cool white shade (3866) and then go back in with three strands of the green shade (580) to finish stitching the ribbons with a longer satin stitch. Finish off the present with the same green shade (580) and a six-stranded lazy daisy stitch for the bows on top (**O**).

14. Fill in the pink wavy flowers in the middle. Start by using the lighter green shade (3053) and a lazy daisy branch stitch to fill out the vines on either side of the wavy flower. Go in with three strands of the light pink shade (223) to fill in the petals of the flower with a wavy petal stitch. Finish off the flowers with the red shade (3721) and a three-stranded satin stitch to fill in the centers of the flowers (**P**). Fill in the other pink flower with the same techniques!

15. Fill in the center candy cane with the cool white (3866) and the darker red (3721) with a three-stranded satin stitch (**Q**).

16. Stitch the star-speckled present. Use three strands of the lighter yellow (739) to satin stitch the base of the present, and then go back in with three strands of the gold shade (435) to back stitch the stars on top. Finish the present by using three strands of the same gold (435) with a lazy daisy stitch to finish the bow on top (**R**).

17. From here you can stitch the polka dotted present. Use three strands of the dark green shade (580) to satin stitch the base of the present, being careful to stitch around the polka dots. Then go back in with three strands of the cool white (3866) to fill in the polka dot shapes with satin stitches. Finish off the present by using six strands of the bright red (3831) and a lazy daisy stitch to fill in the bow (**S**).

18. Now that you've finished stitching in the more vibrant elements in the middle of the stocking, focus on stitching the next holly berry border. Use three strands of the lighter green (3053) and darker green (580) with a holly leaf stitch to fill out the leaves across the border. Take a second to fill in the leaves of the lone holly berry in the middle of the stocking. From here, go in with six-stranded French knots to fill in the berries. Use a combination of the pink and red shades (223, 777) for their respective berries, including the lone holly berry in the middle (**T, U**).

19. Once you've stitched the holly berries, all that's left is to fill in the remaining lighter elements at the top of the stocking. You'll use a lot of the same colours and stitching techniques as you did at the start of the pattern. Use three strands of the cool white (3866) to fill in the white sections of the petals, loopy branches, candy cane stripes, diamond stars, present stripes, and bows (**V**).

20. Go in with three strands of the various shades of green (471, 3053) to fill in the remaining green elements including the leafy vines, pine branches, present stripes, ribbons, and bows (**W**).

21. Use three strands of the lightest shade of yellow (739) with a three-stranded satin leaf stitch and whipped back stitch to fill in the stars (**D**).

22. Lastly, use three strands of the pink shade (223) to fill in the candy cane stripes and hearts at the top (**C**). After all this detailed stitching, you're finally done! Double check to see if you've missed any elements and give yourself a pat on the back.

Christmas Cabin

AS A GIRL WHO'S CELEBRATED EVERY SINGLE CHRISTMAS I can remember in northern Canada with winters full of fluffy white snow, it's always been a dream of mine to spend the coziest holiday in a little wooden cabin with a crackling fire, freshly cut Christmas tree, and all of the holiday magic. I've yet to make the dream a reality, so I thought I would channel it into this festive little Christmas cabin strung up with garlands and a roof full of snow. This pattern is quite a labour of love with the amount of satin stitching, back stitching, and French knots you'll make, but the end result is more than worth it. You can stitch this pattern on whatever item you'd like, but beware that the long satin-stitched strands of the house and snowy base won't fare well with washing on a tea towel or other garment—this pattern is more tailored to being a decorative embroidered artwork. You can even go as far as stretching the fabric base over a hard base after stitching and try framing it as a unique piece of fibre artwork! Please feel free to add any additional embellishments to the trees to make them more festive, including stars, beads, or sequin ornaments!

MATERIALS

- 8" Square of Fabric (I used Kona cotton in the shade Natural)
- Embroidery Floss (see colour guide for suggested hues)
- Embroidery Hoop (6" or 15 cm)
- Embroidery Snips/Scissors
- Pattern Transferring Tools + Transfer Method of Choice
- Size 5 Embroidery Needle

COLOUR GUIDE

- Blanc
- 762
- 644
- 3782
- 839
- 777
- 3072
- 3023
- 3363
- 3362
- 3346
- 3053

STITCH GUIDE

A 3053, satin stitch, 3 strands

B 3072, 644, and 3023, satin stitch, 3 strands

C 762 and 3782, satin stitch, 3 strands

D 839, back stitch and cross knots, 6 strands

E 3363 and 3362, lazy daisy stitch, 3 strands

F 3363, chain stitch, 3 strands

G 777, cross knots, 3 strands

H 3362, chain stitch, 3 strands; 777, chain stitch and back stitch, 3 strands

I Blanc, French knots, 6 strands

J Blanc, satin stitch and whipped back stitch, 3 strands

K 839, satin stitch, 3 strands and long stitch, 6 strands

L 3362 and 3346, back stitch, 6 strands

INSTRUCTIONS

1. Start the cabin by stitching the light-green base. Use three strands of the mint green shade (3053) and a satin stitch to fill in the middle of the house (**A**). You'll want to start at the bottom-right edge of the house (just above the brick) and use long satin stitches to pull your threads up and down the house from the base of the brick to the bottom edges of the garlands. Make sure to also stitch inside the inner parts of the garland (but not the garlands themselves).

TIP for Stitching the Base of the Cabin: Use the satin-stitch method of your choice, but make sure not to pull your strands too tightly, or the fabric and floss will bunch. Run your stitches up and down as far as they will reach, working carefully around the door, windows, shutters, and garlands.

2. Next, fill in the brick with the three muted shades (644, 3072, 3023) with a three-stranded satin stitch (**B**). Start with the stitches on the far left of the house and work your way to the right and around the corner. I found the easiest way to do this was to work on one row at a time, alternating the three colours one after another. Repeat this method again below each row, making sure to stagger the colours so they don't end up next to the same shades. Run a horizontal stitch down the middle of each brick and fill out the edges on either side. Don't forget to also do the bricks on the top of the roof!

3. Next, work on stitching in the windows. Use three strands of the light grey shade (762) to fill the inner panes of the windows. Next, use the lighter brown shade (3782) with a three-stranded satin stitch to fill in the window shutters, running your stitches horizontally (**C**). Once you've done all the windows and shutters, use the brown shade (839) to run six-stranded back stitches over the windows to create the defined square windowpanes (**D**). Don't forget to stitch the outline of the window, up to the garland, and over the shutters too.

4. Continue filling in the house by stitching the door. Use three strands of the lighter brown shade (3782) and longer satin stitches to fill in the door, being mindful to stitch around the wreath outline, but covering the door knob (**C**). Start with a stitch down the middle and work your way out on either side. Finish the door off by using the darker brown shade and a six-stranded cross knot to stitch the door knob overtop and to the right of the door (**D**).

5. Next, stitch in all of the garlands around the door and around the arches of the windows. You'll want to use both green shades (3363, 3362) with three-stranded lazy daisy stitches to fill in the arched garland around the door. Start with three strands of the darker green (3362) and use sporadically placed stitches around the whole door. Then you'll go back in with the same three strands in the lighter green (3363) to fill in the gaps and fully fill in the door's arched garland. Use the same colours (3362, 3363) and method to fill in the arches around the windows, too (**E**). Alternatively, you can just fill in the garlands with one green shade of your choice as well!

6. Continue by using three strands of the lighter green (3363) and a chain stitch to fill in the arched garlands hanging down at the top of the roof (**F**). Start at the bottom-left edge of the roof and use the chain stitches for each curved arch. End your chain stitches at the top of each arch and start again at the top of the next arch. Use this technique to work your way all around the roof.

7. Now you'll use the red shade (777) to add the three-stranded cross-knot berries to all the garlands (**G**). Make sure to alternate the placement of your berries accordingly all across your garlands.

TIP **for Stitching the Cross Knot Berries on the Garlands:** You can add the berries in the gaps around the roof for the garlands on the door and windows, but for the arched garlands, use the cross knots over the chain-stitched loop edges to secure them in place. Simply stitch your first cross knot stitch over the top of one of your loops and cross it again if you'd like a fuller berry.

continued . . .

. . . continued

8. Your next step is to add the chain stitch wreath to the door. Use three strands of the darker green (3362) to chain stitch the wreath around the remaining outline on the door. Then use three strands of the red shade (777) to stitch the bow with a combination of chain stitches and back stitches (**H**).

9. Finish off the house by stitching in the snow on the roof with six strands of the white (Blanc) with French knot stitches (**I**). Start at the bottom-left edge of the narrower slant of the roof and stitch around the outer edges of the entire roof. Then proceed to fill in the rest of the snow on the roof.

TIP **for Stitching the French Knot "Snow" on the Cabin Roof:** I found it easiest to work in inch-by-inch sections as I was filling in the roof, so you can build it up slowly but evenly. Make sure to also take breaks as you're working, as this can be a slow and tedious process! Alternatively, you can also simply fill in the roof with a longer-stranded satin stitch in the same white (Blanc) colour.

10. Next up, you'll work on stitching in the snowy base of the house. Use three strands of the white shade (Blanc) and long satin stitches. Start from the middle and work your way out on either side with your satin stitch method of choice, but make sure not to pull your strands too tightly, or the fabric and floss will bunch. Once you're done, use three strands of the same white (Blanc) and a whipped back stitch to create the border around the snow and edges of the house (**J**).

11. Lastly, finish stitching in the trees to round out the pattern. Start by stitching the tree trunks using the darker brown shade (839) and a three-stranded satin stitch. Use the same brown shade (839) and a six-stranded long stitch for the middle trunk lines of the trees. Then use the same long stitch method to stitch down each of the tree branch bases (**K**).

12. From here you'll take six strands of the darkest green shade (3362) and, starting at the top of the far-right tree, fill in the branches along the grey directional lines with a simple back stitch, all the way down each branch until you've filled out the whole tree. Repeat this method for the other two trees, as well. Afterward, take six strands of the warmer green shade (3346) and use it to fill in the gaps around the branches to fill out the trees and give them more depth (**L**)!

CHAPTER 4

Being Mindful

WHEN I WAS GROWING UP, we often spent Christmas eve at my grandma's house, where she would prepare a feast. We would all sit around the living room with foldable trays by the couch or cross legged on the floor, eating dinner and chatting amongst ourselves. Later in the evening we would open presents together, go around hugging each other in thanks, and just sit with one another in the cozy glow of Christmas eve. As the years have gone by and our family traditions have shifted, the quiet moments spent with loved ones, taking the time to prepare food for one another, and giving thoughtful gifts is what has really resonated with me through the years.

As someone who fully embraces each season (well, maybe not the rest of winter!)—especially each seasonal holiday with all of the décor, themes, and cliché activities, you'll best believe I love the Christmas season and all of the cozy moments that can be found leading up to the end of the year. But at the same time, there can be a lot of whirlwind feelings around the holidays when it comes to who you're spending time with, collecting the perfect gift, or curating the perfect day. Little things like missing loved ones, stretching your budget, and trying to capture Christmas magic can weigh on your heart and take away from the small moments of joy found scattered throughout December.

This is a little reminder to be mindful of how you're spending your time and where you're placing your energy this holiday season. Embroidery is one of those art forms that forces you to slow down and allows you to quiet your mind and reflect on what truly matters. When you take the time to decipher what things bring you joy during the holidays, you might find the answers are in family time, thoughtfulness, and simplicity. Taking the time to catch up with a loved one,

presenting friends and family with handmade gifts, or gathering the ingredients to make a favorite meal can make a world of difference in how you feel about your holiday.

Find some time to slow down and enjoy the coziness of the season with mindful activities like crafting, baking, doing a puzzle, reading a festive novel, or watching a favorite holiday movie. During the bustling days and dark evenings of December, it can make a world of difference when you prioritize putting on your cozy clothes, turning on the Christmas lights, and doing something fun and peaceful.

I'm sending you my personal warmest wishes for the holiday season and want to thank you so much for choosing to make projects from this book, or for choosing to gift them to a loved one this Christmas. I hope it gives you some time to slow down and practice the magic that can be found in creating something with your own two hands!

Happiest Holidays,

—Aly

Acknowledgments

It's been a dream of mine to write a book for a long time now—not in the sense that I'm some great writer that has a million stories just bursting to be told, but because I have a passion for creating and have always wanted to share that passion with others. For a while I wasn't sure what kind of book to write, and even considered illustrating a book rather than writing one, but after starting my embroidery business and writing my own patterns, it felt like the next right topic for publishing a book.

That dream came true when Maggie, my lovely editor, reached out about working on a book of Christmas embroidery patterns with her and the amazing team at Rocky Nook. I owe Maggie a huge thank you for responding to countless emails, being a great sounding board for the publishing process, and making this process a wonderful one.

To the designer of this book, Kim Scott, and compositor Danielle Foster, my endless gratitude for the thoughtfulness and care you've put into designing these pages. I can't express how grateful I am to have my ideas and feedback heard and to have created this project together. Thank you also to everybody at Rocky Nook for believing in me and cheering me on in the making of *Handmade Holiday*—you guys are a gift to creative individuals everywhere.

To my parents, thank you for your endless support and faith in me throughout my whole life. I can't remember a single day when you didn't encourage me to create and beamed at every piece of artwork (good or bad) I've ever produced. It means the world to me to have two parents who believe in my entrepreneurship whole-heartedly and take every chance they can to brag about their talented, artistic, self-employed daughter. I'm forever grateful to my cheerleaders for life and for their unconditional love. And to my little brother, thank you for pushing me to live up to my best self.

Thanks also to all of my grandparents for passing down the best parts of themselves that live on in me today. To my Grandpa Ploof for his love of gardening and being outdoors. To my Grandma Ploof for the joy of working with my hands, and for always pinning up my artwork on her refrigerator. To my Grandma Brian for my passion for homemaking, and love of nature and sewing. And to my Grandpa Brian for my appreciation for peace and quiet and taking the time to slow down. You all had an endless supply of love and belief in me, and it's shaped me into the person I am today.

To my Aunties S & H, thank you for inspiring me to create through your own creative pursuits and for always stocking me up with a rainbow of art supplies. You've always met my creative pursuits with encouraging words and that means a lot coming from family.

To my Triple M Best Friends, thank you for always cheering me on in all of my artistic endeavors and for being by my side for some huge milestones. You guys are my favorite people to be around and gosh knows many of my artworks hang proudly in your homes. I owe a debt of thanks to you for always inspiring me with your own creative outlets and always mentioning my name in a room of opportunities.

To AB, for being the bestie who will always bring peace and comfort into my life. You've

been a cheerleader of mine for years and it means so much when you always meet my wins and worries with a thoughtful response and an encouraging outlook.

To S & B, thank you for always hyping up my artistic endeavors and for being proud of my small business wins. You guys were there from the start and no matter where our careers take us, I know we'll always cheer each other on.

A special thanks to the arts and embroidery communities and all of my fellow artist and embroidery friends for a constant source of support, inspiration, and comradery. When you spend hours upon hours working on a new artwork, there's no better validation then that of your peers.

And to all of the wonderful followers and fellow creatives around the world who support me, my business, and my artistic career, an enormous thank you. You've made quite a few dreams of mine a reality and I can't express how much it means to have a community of people to pass along that passion for creating to. I hope you love this book as much as I loved creating it!

About the Author

Alyssa, or Aly as she is known by her friends and followers, has been artistically inclined her entire life. She has a keen affinity for colour palettes, textures, and shapes and has pursued many a creative outlet. She originally started out with drawing portraits and later took painting lessons in her spare time, but she is primarily self-taught. Aly even went as far as pursuing post-secondary education in the fine arts and interior design fields, but continued to pursue her passion for creating in her spare time.

In 2021, she stitched her first embroidery artwork when the world had slowed down and discovered a whole new love for the fibre art form. She adored the textural aspects of the satiny floss and soft linen and put her past assets of free-hand drawing and colour theory to good use in creating original designs. After finishing her first hoop, Aly was inspired to explore the embroidery world further and found a wealth of information and inspiration on social media. She started posting her works to her own artistry

Instagram account (@byalyploof) and slowly grew a following of friends and fellow creators. She also opened an Etsy shop under the same name and posted a few of her original embroidery artworks and her first digital embroidery PDF pattern at the end of 2021. Her dad was her very first customer and bought several of her original hoops for the neighbors as Christmas gifts. It was a humbling experience for Aly, but everybody has to start somewhere, right?

Jump forward a few years to present day and you'll find that Aly's small business and social media have flourished quite a bit. She's grown her online community to well over 170k+ and has also published many more original patterns to her shop, in addition to launching several holiday collections. She is incredibly grateful for the community of creative individuals who collect and stitch her patterns and is eternally grateful for the opportunity to live out her dreams of creating for a living.

Owning and running her small business has afforded her the chance to wear many hats, including: production artist, supply manager, product photographer, pattern writer, bookkeeper, marketing specialist, and social media manager. Aly adores photography and editing and shoots all of her own product photos,

including over 95% of the photos in this book (excluding the photos of herself, which she credits to her mom/assistant photographer extraordinaire). She also has a bit of a social media addiction, which she has turned into a helpful marketing tool for her small business. At any given point, you might see her hunched over an iPhone tripod trying to film a 10-second reel to share on her Instagram page.

Aly has always been drawn to nature and floral motifs; from the time that she was doodling flowers in her high school notebooks to present day, when she doodles flowers to create unique embroidery designs, you can certainly attribute florals to being a permanent element in Aly's brand and business. She's a nature lover through and through, and deems it a point of pride to take inspiration from the world around her and transform that joy into her designs.

Aly was born and currently lives with her family in the Canadian city of Edmonton, Alberta. In her free time, you can find her taking a million photos of random flowers, travelling the world with her friends and family, baking and cooking to her heart's content, reading in the bathtub for hours on end, and swooning over all of the regency-era romance series.

Pattern Templates

Stitch Sampler

TRACEABLE PATTERN TEMPLATE

Reminder! This pattern is to scale. For best results, center it in your hoop when tracing.
The light-grey directional lines can be fully traced or simply referenced when stitching.

Poinsanta Hat

TRACEABLE PATTERN TEMPLATE

Reminder! This pattern is to scale. For best results, center it in your hoop when tracing.
The light-grey directional lines can be fully traced or simply referenced when stitching.

Cup of Christmas

TRACEABLE PATTERN TEMPLATE

Reminder! This pattern is to scale. For best results, center it in your hoop when tracing.
The light-grey directional lines can be fully traced or simply referenced when stitching.

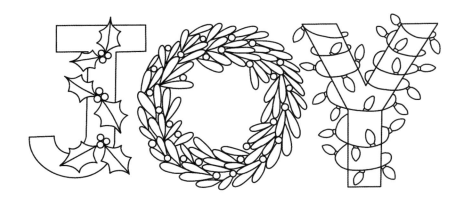

TRACEABLE PATTERN TEMPLATE

Reminder! This pattern is to scale. For best results, center it in your hoop when tracing.
The light-grey directional lines can be fully traced or simply referenced when stitching.

Scarves and Snowflakes

TRACEABLE PATTERN TEMPLATE

Reminder! This pattern is to scale. For best results, center it in your hoop when tracing.
The light-grey directional lines can be fully traced or simply referenced when stitching.

Merry Mittens

TRACEABLE PATTERN TEMPLATE

Reminder! This pattern is to scale. For best results, center it in your hoop when tracing.
The light-grey directional lines can be fully traced or simply referenced when stitching.

Starry Stockings

TRACEABLE PATTERN TEMPLATE

Reminder! This pattern is to scale. For best results, center it in your hoop when tracing.
The light-grey directional lines can be fully traced or simply referenced when stitching.

Bells and Beads

TRACEABLE PATTERN TEMPLATE

Reminder! This pattern is to scale. For best results, center it in your hoop when tracing.
The light-grey directional lines can be fully traced or simply referenced when stitching.

Holiday Rocking Horse

TRACEABLE PATTERN TEMPLATE

Reminder! This pattern is to scale. For best results, center it in your hoop when tracing.
The light-grey directional lines can be fully traced or simply referenced when stitching.

Rainbow Snow Globe

TRACEABLE PATTERN TEMPLATE

Reminder! This pattern is to scale. For best results, center it in your hoop when tracing.
The light-grey directional lines can be fully traced or simply referenced when stitching.

Pretty Poinsettia

TRACEABLE PATTERN TEMPLATE

Reminder! This pattern is to scale. For best results, center it in your hoop when tracing.
The light-grey directional lines can be fully traced or simply referenced when stitching.

Citrus and Berries

TRACEABLE PATTERN TEMPLATE

*Reminder! This pattern is to scale. For best results, center it in your hoop when tracing.
The light-grey directional lines can be fully traced or simply referenced when stitching.*

Candy Cane Blooms

TRACEABLE PATTERN TEMPLATE

Reminder! This pattern is to scale. For best results, center it in your hoop when tracing.
The light-grey directional lines can be fully traced or simply referenced when stitching.

Feathers and Florals

TRACEABLE PATTERN TEMPLATE

Reminder! This pattern is to scale. For best results, center it in your hoop when tracing.
The light-grey directional lines can be fully traced or simply referenced when stitching.

Bows and Baubles

TRACEABLE PATTERN TEMPLATE

Reminder! This pattern is to scale. For best results, center it in your hoop when tracing.
The light-grey directional lines can be fully traced or simply referenced when stitching.

Stuffed Stocking

TRACEABLE PATTERN TEMPLATE

Reminder! This pattern is to scale. For best results, center it in your hoop when tracing.
The light-grey directional lines can be fully traced or simply referenced when stitching.

Christmas Cabin

TRACEABLE PATTERN TEMPLATE

Reminder! This pattern is to scale. For best results, center it in your hoop when tracing.
The light-grey directional lines can be fully traced or simply referenced when stitching.